magical
candle
crafting

About the Author

Ember Grant has been practicing the Craft for over ten years. Since 2003, she has been contributing to *Llewellyn's Witches' Calendar*, *Llewellyn's Spell-A-Day Almanac*, and *Llewellyn's Magical Almanac*, and has published articles in *PanGaia*, *newWitch*, and *Circle Magazine*. A poet and photographer as well, Ember's work explores nature, spirituality, folklore, and mythology. She lives in Missouri. Visit her online at EmberGrant.com.

To Write to the Author

If you wish to contact the author or would like more information about this book, please write to the author in care of Llewellyn Worldwide and we will forward your request. Both the author and publisher appreciate hearing from you and learning of your enjoyment of this book and how it has helped you. Llewellyn Worldwide cannot guarantee that every letter written to the author can be answered, but all will be forwarded. Please write to:

Ember Grant
℅ Llewellyn Worldwide
2143 Wooddale Drive
Woodbury, MN 55125-2989, U.S.A.
Please enclose a self-addressed stamped envelope for reply,
or $1.00 to cover costs. If outside the U.S.A., enclose
an international postal reply coupon.

Many of Llewellyn's authors have websites with additional information and resources. For more information, please visit our website at:

www.llewellyn.com

magical candle crafting

CREATE YOUR OWN CANDLES FOR SPELLS & RITUALS

EMBER GRANT

Llewellyn Publications
Woodbury, Minnesota

First Edition
Second Printing, 2014

Cover design by Kevin R. Brown
Cover images: flower petals and spices © PhotoDisc; herbs © Digital Stock
Interior illustrations by Llewellyn Art Department
Editing by Nicole Edman

Llewellyn is a registered trademark of Llewellyn Worldwide Ltd.

Library of Congress Cataloging-in-Publication Data
Grant, Ember, 1971–
  Magical candle crafting : create your own candles for spells & rituals /
by Ember Grant.
       p. cm.
  Includes bibliographical references and index.
  ISBN 978-0-7387-2135-4
  1. Candle making. 2. Candles and lights. I. Title.
  TT896.5.G74 2011
  745.593'3—dc22
                         2010027699

Note: The techniques described in this book involve some elements that may pose safety risks, including stoves, hot water, and heated wax. Please proceed with caution and common sense. If necessary, seek assistance. The publisher is not liable for any harm incurred while engaging in candle making.

Llewellyn Worldwide Ltd. does not participate in, endorse, or have any authority or responsibility concerning private business transactions between our authors and the public.
  All mail addressed to the author is forwarded, but the publisher cannot, unless specifically instructed by the author, give out an address or phone number.
  Any Internet references contained in this work are current at publication time, but the publisher cannot guarantee that a specific location will continue to be maintained. Please refer to the publisher's website for links to authors' websites and other sources.

Llewellyn Publications
A Division of Llewellyn Worldwide Ltd.
2143 Wooddale Drive
Woodbury, MN 55125-2989
www.llewellyn.com

Printed in the United States of America

For Ellen—
Without your encouragement, this book would remain unwritten.

Contents

Candle Recipes

Introduction

No facts are to me sacred; none are profane;
I simply experiment, an endless seeker....

—RALPH WALDO EMERSON

Consider everything that was made possible by the discovery of fire—cooking, warmth, light—and how that discovery has progressed over time to change our lives. Fire is sacred to us, though we most likely take it for granted in the modern world we live in. I invite you to return to honoring a sacred flame—the fire of the home, of life, of spirituality. Candles can be used to celebrate every aspect of our lives and to enrich our world with magic. They offer us just enough light to see yet still maintain the mystery of darkness—a soft, gentle glow that can be both comforting and powerful.

The goal of this book is to help you create your own candles for magical use, candles infused with your personal energy and intent. In addition, you will learn how to recycle used wax, which is more economical and environmentally friendly than buying new candles. Once you've had some practice with these recipes and spells, you'll be able to create your own votive candles and truly personalize your candle magic. I think you'll find that the personal touch makes all the difference.

What Is Magic?

Magic is a word that carries a lot of weight and often a lot of excess baggage. Its definition changes throughout time and across cultures, giving it a vast spectrum of meanings. For the purpose of this book, magic is the craft practiced by Wiccans, modern Witches, and those following other Neo-Pagan spiritual paths, as well as some New Age practitioners. And even among these people there are undoubtedly many different ideas about what magic is.

One definition of magic is that it's a way of focusing the mind to bring about change. For others, it's about transcending to another way of seeing and experiencing the world. Magic can also be a way to engage one's imagination with a personal set of beliefs in order to fully experience the extraordinary and beautiful mysteries of life.

So then, you might ask, is magic spiritual? It can be. Many feel that spells are something akin to prayer, although instead of simply asking deity for help, the practitioner is taking a more active role. I believe spells can involve requesting the assistance of both deity without and deity within—the divine spirits you choose to honor as well as the divine spirit inside you. You are acknowledging your connection with the world around you. All nature is sacred and filled with the divine spark of energy, of life. The energy of the universe is divine, and you are part of that energy. Magic taps into this power. Magic, wishes, spells, and prayers basically work along the same principles. When most people pray, they're asking an outside deity for guidance. With magic, you call upon the inner deity as well. We are all spiritual beings, and we all have power. Believing is the first step. If you think your magic will fail, then it will. Faith is at the root of real magic.

Now, more than ever, people are exploring alternate spiritual paths, combining Eastern and Western traditions into an eclectic blend of personal preferences. Just look at the New Age, Metaphysical, and Occult sections of the local bookstore. Twenty years ago, even though those beliefs were present, the materials were not nearly as accessible. And the Internet has brought information to seekers as never before. If it all seems more prevalent now, perhaps it's because the more we advance technologically, the more we crave some basic, imaginative connection and experience. But remember, dabbling shallowly in a large pool is ultimately not as satisfying as finding depth in a few places. I urge you to explore all those areas that interest you, then take on serious study in the subjects that speak to you most sincerely.

Even though this book has been written with modern Witches, Wiccans, and Neo-Pagans in mind, anyone of any spiritual path can create magic. If the word *magic* doesn't appeal to you, think of it as prayer or positive affirmation. Before reading this book, you may have considered magic the stuff of fairy tales. I hope that after you have had success with the spells included here, you'll see magic in a new light.

I believe magic, in whatever form, is with us to stay. Human beings are wired for spiritual experience. Scientific studies have shown that our brains are activated by altered states such as meditation and trance, indicating that spirituality and magic are perfectly understandable needs, if not for everyone, at least for what seems to be a majority. And for those with imagination—the seekers and those who crave a mystical experience and connection with mystery—explore magic. See where it takes you.

A Brief History of Candles

We all know that candles and candlelight are an important part of family and cultural traditions such as birthdays, holidays, and special celebrations. Candles incite romance, relaxation, and peace. They inspire us and make our surroundings beautiful, both indoors and out. But we must not forget that candles began as a purely practical tool—they provided light in the darkness. Just imagine the very discovery of fire itself. That changed the lives of humans forever! The tiniest flicker of flame must have seemed as sacred as the life-giving sun.

In the Middle Ages, candles were originally made of rendered animal fat (tallow). These candles were greasy and possessed an unpleasant odor. There were other ways to make candles, but those methods were far more costly. The Romans prized beeswax, a byproduct of honey, for its cleanliness, long burn time, and aroma, but it was expensive. Candles could also be made from vegetable wax, but these could not be produced on a large scale.

However, we resourceful humans found a way to improve things. In the 1800s, candles began to change. Stearin, a waxy solid found in animal and vegetable fats and oils, was added to candles to increase firmness and give them a longer burning time and a more pleasant odor. Soon after, paraffin wax was used for candles. This wax is a byproduct of the petroleum-refining industry. Most candles today are a combination of ingredients such as paraffin, natural waxes, and beeswax. The paraffin sold in stores for candle making usually has stearic acid (stearin) added. (Just be sure you don't buy the wax from the grocery store that is used for canning—it won't work for making candles.)

The magical candles described in this book are plain and practical. No one will see these candles but you (with a few exceptions). However, you can easily decorate some to give as gifts or for use in a ritual when you'd like them to look prettier—or you can simply use candleholders. Craft stores carry a wide range of supplies and books that can help you make beautiful and creative candles, if you choose to pursue candle making as a hobby. But this book does not address decorative candles, beyond "dressing up" these simple candles just a bit.

As with any kind of magic, the more personal your effort, the better the results will be. This is why creating your own candles makes such a difference—you can focus energy while making the candle as well as when you light it. You could use a store-bought candle and focus intent when you burn it—this is still magic. But your spells will be more effective if you also empower the wax from scratch, in its molten form.

Our energy, life force, the complexities of our brain and subconscious mind, and our body are amazing miracles of nature. If the universe and all it encompasses are considered divine, you may wonder if this includes human-made objects. The answer is yes. As you will discover, when you make something, it becomes special. That's the magic of hand-made candles.

1 How to Make Candles

Religion is a candle inside a multicolored lantern.
Everyone looks through a particular color, but the candle
is always there.

—MOHAMMED NAGUIB

Candle crafting is an old tradition with various methods and styles. For the purpose of creating a magical candle, however, we'll keep the process as simple as possible. The goal is to create a candle that is time- and cost-effective, with a process that is so easy it becomes second nature. This way you'll have more energy to focus on the magical aspects.

The Personal Touch

There's nothing wrong with buying candles for your spiritual or magical use. People do it every day. But when you want a candle for a specific purpose, it can be difficult to find the perfect combination of qualities that you need. Rather than buying a candle, you can make it yourself and create a suitable candle with your particular goals in mind. Your energy and focus are part of the creative process from the start, making your hand-made candle far more special than any you could purchase. You don't have to be concerned about the finished product being perfect—we aren't making candles to look at, we're making them to burn. This is a practical side of magic—a useful, functional, and magical creation. It's all about intent.

In addition, we enjoy homemade items for the same reason that eating frozen pizza or restaurant food fails to satisfy after you eat it too often. Sometimes you just want a home-cooked meal of food prepared with care. Like a big family pot-luck, a gift of homemade brownies from a friend, or a birthday cake baked just for you, there's something special about items we make ourselves or those made by someone close to us. Sometimes we have to settle for convenience, but the experience is always nicer when the item has been carefully prepared by hand. The same goes for craft items. Soaps, candles, flower arrangements, greeting cards—a hand-made gift truly possesses a personal touch. As the old saying goes, "It's the thought that counts." In the case of magic, those words are profound.

For example, you can go into a grocery store and buy a loaf of bread created in a factory by machines. The human element is far removed here. The bread may still be good, and even healthy, but the personal touch is missing. It's OK for everyday sandwiches, but imagine you're having a dinner party and you want something special. So you try a local bakery. You may even know the owners and employees. You know they make everything by hand and the product is fresh, baked that morning. It's more personal, a nicer touch. But it would be even better if you baked that bread yourself—this way you would know every ingredient being put into it; your time, energy, and love have gone into that bread, and those who eat it can tell. When you say to your guests, "I made it myself," the response is always one of appreciation. The fact that you took the time shows you care. That's the personal, human element that takes place in creating a magical craft. This makes the item special.

The Candle Kitchen

You can make candles anywhere, but the kitchen is the most practical place. Most of the items you need can already be found there.

Items Needed

- large metal pot (an old soup pot works best; I use a 4- or 5-quart pot that has handles on each side)
- glass carafe (an old coffee pot is ideal) or soup/coffee cans
- candy or candle-making thermometer★
- small paper cups (such as Dixie brand) or other molds
- wax (left over from old candles or purchased new)
- wicks (available at craft stores)

Other Supplies

- wooden spoon
- oven mitt
- old towels, paper towels, newspaper, or waxed paper
- herbs, resins, essential oils, etc.

★ A candle-making thermometer is marked with the proper pouring temperature for specific candles, but it's not necessary to have this—the candy thermometer works just as well, as long as you know what temperature you need. For most of these candles, the best pouring temperature is 160 degrees F for plastic molds or paper cups; a slightly higher temperature can be used for metal molds. Wax temperature should never be allowed to reach or exceed 300 degrees F.

Gather tools you can dedicate solely to creating candles, since once you start, these items won't be suitable for other use.

Candle making is easy and a fairly clean process. All we're doing is taking wax, melting it down, pouring it into molds, and letting it cool. At a certain time we add a wick. It's really that simple. Keep in mind you'll need plenty of stable surface area for your candles to sit undisturbed while they cool, or use a cookie sheet that you can move to a safe area.

CAUTION: NEVER try to melt wax in a saucepan or in the microwave! It can catch on fire. ALWAYS use the double-boiler method.

Once you have all the tools, you just need wax and wicks. Nearly every craft store sells candle-making supplies, or you can purchase them online. Candle making is very popular, so you should have no trouble finding everything you need.

Please read this section before moving on to the step-by-step instructions. Knowing the mechanics of candle making is important.

The Wax

Walk the aisles of a large craft store and you'll find an endless array of candle-making supplies and products—colors, scents, molds, and project books. For our purposes, we're only going to concern ourselves with wax and wicks. Basically, wax is fuel. This is how a candle burns.

The basic method for a beginner is to start by purchasing a large block of uncolored wax. Small blocks of colored wax are also sold and can be melted along with the uncolored wax to achieve your desired result. This is one area where keeping the remains of spent candles can save you some money. Rather than buying colored chunks of wax, you can just add pieces of an old candle to the uncolored wax.

If you have enough old candles lying around, you can make your candles entirely from recycled wax, which is what I've been doing for years. Friends also save their spent candle wax for me, and I can't recall the last time I had to purchase candle wax from a store.

The purpose of making recycled candles is to use of all those scraps of wax left over from old candles, and to save money. If you don't have a lot of old wax right now, start saving it. Have your friends and relatives save theirs for you and soon you'll have more wax than you can use! Until then, just buy blocks of wax. For votive candles, purchase wax that is made for molded candles (as opposed to wax designed to be poured into a glass jar—we'll discuss that later).

Using recycled wax from spent candles is a bit of an adventure. Since wax quality varies, one good way for beginners to get started is to take one very large candle that has burned down, such as the large three-wick type, and make many smaller votives from it.

If you have many different shades of a color, it's fine to mix them all together. You'll still get a nice, even tone. You can also experiment with mixing different colors. If you need an orange candle, try mixing red and yellow wax. Or, if you want purple but only have a small chunk of purple wax, use white wax and add a few chunks of the purple wax to color it. You can also mix purchased wax (especially beeswax) with used candles to get a more even-burning candle.

A good rule to follow when using recycled wax is to create the same type of candle as the wax came from. If the wax came from a molded candle, it should be fine to create new molded candles. If it came from a container like a glass jar, it will be a softer wax, so you should mix it with a harder wax if you plan to make a molded candle. Container wax from a jar candle has a lower melting point. You can pour this type into another container if you wish, but I've found that doesn't work as well. If you'd like to try container candles, it's best to purchase wax made especially for that purpose and follow the directions on the package. (Also remember you can reuse glass candle containers for burning votives or tea lights; just clean out the wax using the water method as directed later in this chapter, and wash the jar.)

The wax chunks should be fairly small for quicker melting—approximately 2 inches in diameter or less. A good way to break up large blocks of wax is to place the wax in a plastic bag and use a hammer to break it. This is best done on a hard surface, such as the concrete floor of a garage. You may want to place a mat or rug on the floor—you don't want to accidentally crack your concrete!

You can experiment with the amount of wax you melt at one time. When using a standard-size coffee carafe, fill it just over halfway with wax chunks. When they melt down, you should have enough wax to fill several paper cups. Eventually, you'll become comfortable with the amount of wax that yields a certain number of candles. Don't worry about measuring. The tiny amount of ingredients called for in these candles won't be affected by the amount of wax. You will most likely be making these candles in batches, not singly. However, depending on the molds you use, your batch may yield fewer candles.

Other Types of Wax

Soy wax is also available and burns cleaner than other types; however, it's very soft, so it should be used to create a container candle, not a molded one. Beeswax sheets are another easy way to make your own candles quickly—you just roll them up with a wick inside and they're ready to burn. But these styles don't allow for the same level of creativity in adding spell ingredients. However, adding some beeswax to other types of wax will make for a better-quality molded candle.

I prefer the standard melting method of candle making—it provides a recycling opportunity and includes the added bonus of stirring a bubbling cauldron!

The Wick

There are several types of wicking. You can buy long strips that can be cut to a specific size, which come in braided or wire (metal core). The metal core is safe (lead isn't used anymore) and it's what holds up best for molded candles. Braided wicking is soft and is best used for dipping taper candles. Wick tabs are small metal plates that you can crimp to the bottom of your wick to help the wick stand up, but they are not necessary for this type of candle and method. Another easy method if you're making votive candles is to buy wicks that have tabs already attached to the bottom. These are perfect for paper cup candles. You'll probably get about a dozen in a package, so it's cheaper to buy the long length of wicking and cut it, but the choice is yours. Sometimes wicks with tabs are useful, as you'll see in some of the spell candle recipes. These pre-tabbed wicks are primed (coated with wax to make them stand straight) but you can easily do this yourself by simply dipping your wicking into molten wax and laying it down to dry.

There are generally three wick sizes: small, medium, and large. The packages indicate what candle size each is used for. Paper cup size is about 1½ to 2 inches in diameter, so small or medium wicking works best for these candles. Ideally, your candle will burn evenly all the way down. If you use wicking that's too large, you may end up with a runny mess; wicking that is too small will cause the candle to burn down in the middle but leave an outer shell. This may be a desired effect since there's less chance of a mess. (Keep in mind that a hole could form in the shell and liquid wax could still spill through.)

Medium wicking is the best choice for the paper cup votive. However, you still may not get perfect burning, especially when using recycled wax. Be prepared for your candle to burn crookedly or the wax to be softer or harder than you expect. When mixing wax, you never know what results you'll get, so always burn these types of candles in a safe container.

The Mold

These recipes simply require a small paper cup, such as Dixie brand, to create a basic votive candle. Just about any container that can withstand heat can be used for a mold, but remember: you have to be able to get the candle out. This can be difficult. That's why paper cups work so well—you just peel them off. Of course, you can invest in reusable molds that are sold at craft stores, but keep in mind that you'll need lots of them to pour many candles at once. Sometimes I like to use an old cardboard juice can. They're easy to peel and make a larger, longer-burning candle. You can also try using a metal mini-muffin pan to make small floating candles. Just rub a little cooking oil in the cups and, after the wax has cooled, pop the pan in the freezer for a few minutes to make the candles easier to release.

Craft stores sell metal votive and tea light molds that are reusable and produce a nice, smooth finish. Basically you should make the decision based on how many candles you want to pour at one time. If you want to invest in molds of this type, you can find "six-pack" votive and tea light molds for multiple pouring. They will cost more than singles but are probably worth the investment. However, one box of paper cups is just a few dollars and can last for years, depending on how often you make candles, so don't let lack of molds stop you from getting started.

To release a candle from a metal votive cup, place the hardened candle in the freezer for about 30 minutes. It should easily slip out of the mold. Don't leave it in the freezer too long or the candle will crack! Many of the larger metal molds require a different process for inserting the wick since these molds are open on the bottom. Such molds also require a special sealing process. You can find plastic molds that snap together—just be sure you fasten the pieces together securely or the wax will leak out. Molds that you purchase from craft stores usually come with specific instructions for use.

With all that said, I have found the paper cup method to be the simplest way to begin, so I will proceed with this method in mind.

Creating the Candle

Step One: Preparation

First, cover the area you'll be using with waxed paper or newspaper to aid in cleanup. Wax will easily scrape off most surfaces after it cools, but cleanup is faster if you don't have to do that. Also, be aware of any fabrics you're using or wearing during the process—splattered wax is more difficult to remove from cloth, although it can sometimes be done using an iron on low heat to melt the wax and blotting it with a damp cloth. Play it safe and wear old clothes (or an apron), and use old towels. I also like to use a cookie sheet to set the candles on to cool, just in case a mold springs a leak or gets tipped over.

Make sure you have all your tools and supplies at hand before you begin.

Step Two: Melting

Add a couple inches of warm tap water to your pot and place it on the stove or hot plate. Put the chunks of wax in the carafe and place the carafe inside the pot of water. This simulates a double boiler. **CAUTION: NEVER try to melt wax in a saucepan or in the microwave! It can catch on fire. ALWAYS use the double-boiler method.**

Turn the burner on medium-high heat. After the water starts to boil, you can turn it down. Try to avoid water splashing up into the wax.

Use the candy thermometer (or special candle-making thermometer) to monitor the temperature of the wax; 160 degrees F is a good average pouring temperature. If your thermometer has a clip, you can attach it to the side of the carafe or can. Be careful not to let the pot boil dry; add water as needed. Remember to stir the wax occasionally while it's melting. **Do not allow the pot to boil dry of water, as the glass carafe could crack or shatter.**

If you'd like to make several different colors at one time, and your pot is large enough, use metal soup or coffee cans. Squeeze one side of the can to make a point for easy pouring. Remember, the cans will get hot, so use your oven mitt when handling them. This way you can make one or two votives in several different colors at once. Watch cans carefully in the water, as they are lighter than a carafe and may float or tip over. You may need to keep your water level a bit lower, but still don't let the pot boil dry.

Step Three: The Wicks

While you're waiting for the wax to melt, cut your wicks to the appropriate length, a little taller than the rim of the cup (or a little taller than your desired candle height—you don't have to completely fill the cup if you want just a little candle). If your wicks are not already waxed, carefully dip the wicks into your fully melted wax so all but the tip you're holding is immersed, then lay them on waxed paper or a cookie sheet to dry. This is called priming the wicks and makes them stiff and easier to work with. They will dry within minutes.

Step Four: Adding Ingredients

When the wax reaches pouring temperature (160 degrees F), it is time to add the spell ingredients. Remove the carafe from the water and place it on a heat-proof surface. According to the specific spell, sprinkle in a few bits of dried herb, resin, or drops of essential oil. Now is the time to do any chants or visualizations you desire. Details and specific spells will be discussed in future chapters.

Stir the molten wax to evenly distribute the ingredients. Ingredients are added immediately before pouring because prolonged heat will diminish the scent and potency of the oils.

Step Five: Pouring

After you have added your special ingredients and stirred, and you have completed visualizations for a specific spell, pour the liquid wax into your molds. Use caution when pouring to prevent wax from dripping or catching fire on the burner. Always wipe the lip of the carafe or can after pouring and remember to wear your oven mitt. As I mentioned earlier, I have found it helpful when using cans to squeeze one side of the can into a point to make pouring easier. Be sure to re-serve some liquid wax and keep it warm, as it will be needed later to "top off" the candles.

NOTE: If you want a full-sized votive and you're using a paper cup, don't fill the cup completely full with the first pour. Remember that you'll be topping off the candle gradually, so leave some room at the top so it doesn't overflow. In addi-tion, you can make smaller candles by only filling the cup halfway.

Step Six: Adding the Wicks and Cooling

Wait about 20 minutes, or until the wax in the molds begins to form a thin "skin" on top, and then stick the wick down into the wax; even without a wick tab it will adhere to the bottom of the cup, where the wax is beginning to thicken. Make sure your wick is centered. If the wick starts to lean, you can place a pencil across the top of the cup so the wick has something to lean against. As the candles cool, a well will probably form around the wick. This is normal, since wax shrinks as it cools. Simply use a fork or toothpick to poke a few holes in the well near the wick and pour a thin layer of wax over the top. Repeat this process as desired until the candles are cool and nearly level on top of the candle. The entire process could take several hours to complete. Of course, if you don't care how the candle looks, don't worry about achieving a near-level surface. I do recommend topping it off at least once, since the wick could lean over later if you don't. Try to keep the wax a consistent temperature during the topping off process; the pouring temperature can change the finished texture of the wax.

When cooling your candles, the general rule is the longer cooling time, the better. Be aware that the outside of the cup may feel cool to the touch but the wax inside may still be soft. Your candles may appear to be "done" within an hour, but rest assured they'll still be soft! It's best to let them sit at least 24 hours before using them. Of course, the larger the candle, the longer it will take to completely harden. For all types mentioned in this book, 24 hours should be sufficient. When the candles are cool, carefully peel off the paper cup. Trim the wick to about ¼ inch above the wax and it's ready to burn! Remember: wax is very forgiving. You can always melt it down and start over if you don't like your finished candles. Also keep in mind that these candles are not designed to look like perfect store-bought candles. They're unique and magical. If you want to create fancier-looking candles, we'll discuss decorations and designs in Chapter 10.

Cleanup

You shouldn't need to wash your carafe and cans, just wipe them with a paper towel after pouring out all the wax. Bits of wick still left in recycled candles may have sunk to the bottom of the carafe, and these can be discarded. Any leftover molten wax can be poured into a paper cup to cool and use in the future. These leftover chunks make good color additives for clear or white wax.

Safety Tips

If a wax fire occurs while you are pouring your candles, immediately turn off the stove and use a damp cloth to cover the pan. You can also use a lid, but be careful to slide the lid on—don't set it directly down on top of the flames since the air could force the fire up and around your hand. Don't use flour or water on a wax fire. You could use baking soda, or a fire extinguisher. Be sure to have a plan in case a fire does occur.

Never pour hot wax down a sink drain—always pour leftover wax into a container. If you get hot wax on your skin, apply cold water. Peel off the wax and treat the burn with a cold compress. See a doctor or go to the emergency room if the burn is severe or covers more than 2 inches of skin.

Safe Burning

These paper cup votives are slightly larger than standard votive candles, so they may not fit in all containers designed to hold votives. Choose a container that allows for some space around the candle. Glass containers are best, but you can use other heat-proof containers as well. Using unique containers to burn your candles can add a new dimension to your magic. Visit antique shops and second-hand stores to find inexpensive and unusual containers. I like to use a tall glass jar or burn several candles on a plate or platter. Don't just set a candle on a tabletop or area where the wax could run freely. And of course, never leave a burning candle unattended. Always check to see that your candle has burned all the way out. Sometimes candles can be deceiving. In a room with other lights on, you may think a candle has burned out when, in fact, there's still a tiny flame. Use special caution when burning your hand-made recycled candles, since they may burn differently than you expect. And don't forget—you can put a smaller container inside a larger one for a unique effect. More tips on magical burning will be given in future chapters.

Storing Your Candles

You may find it useful to have a special box to store your candles. A shoe box works nicely. I have an old jewelry case made of cedar that I also use to store candles (cedar wood is reputed to have protective properties)—it only holds about eight votives, so I save this for candles that are already charged for a spell. I keep the others in a shoe box. If you'd like, you can decorate your box with magical symbols or decorative paper.

Be sure to label your candles right away so you don't forget their purpose. It may be a year before they're used, and by that time you may forget if the candle was charged with a specific spell or not, especially if you made a large batch and several colors.

Now that you know the basics, let's create magical candles!

2

Making Magic

The awakening of awe is the key.

—JOSEPH CAMPBELL

People have been burning candles as a part of spiritual practice for centuries. According to most dictionaries, the adjective *votive* means something offered to fulfill a pledge, or something that expresses a wish. When people say, "I'll light a candle for you," it usually means something like "I'm thinking of you," or "I'll pray for you," or "I'm sending good wishes to you."

But is this really *magic*? It can be.

To understand why candle magic works and how to use it, first you must learn the basics of magical practice—raising and releasing energy, visualization, and intent. These skills work together to make successful magic. If you are already a practitioner of magic, you will still find relevant information in this chapter. If you are unfamiliar with magic, I have included some introductory material to help make it immediately accessible—practice will deepen your experience. Once learned, your candle magic will be especially powerful, and you can apply these skills to other magical workings as well.

Energy

One of the most basic aspects of creating magic is the raising and releasing of energy toward a purpose or goal. Think of energy like power, or fuel—it can come from many sources. Dancing is a form of raising energy. So is singing, making music, or even daydreaming (more about visualization later). In simple terms, energy is a form of using fuel. When you eat, your body burns the food in order to function. The sun is our ultimate source of energy—it feeds plants and is even used for power. Wind can be channeled into energy as well. And, of course, fire is also a kind of energy.

Wiccan author Scott Cunningham gives a three-fold definition of power: there is personal power, Earth power, and divine power. Personal power is the life force within us. We absorb energy from the sun and from foods we eat, and we release it during the everyday activities of our existence. Earth power comes from our planet and natural items such as stones, trees, and flowers. Divine power is the universal life force that has created everything in existence—so your personal power and the power of the Earth are both manifestations of the Divine. Cunningham describes magic as the act of arousing your personal power and directing it toward a goal. The acts of raising, releasing, and directing energy are important in working magic. In *Wicca: A Guide for the Solitary Practitioner*, Cunningham writes that "magic is the projection of natural energies to produce needed effects." (If you're a beginner interested in Wicca, I highly recommend reading *Wicca*.)

Raising energy with candle magic is two-fold: you project energy into the candle when you create it, and you release that energy when you light the candle for a spell or ritual.

There are many ways of raising and releasing energy. Candle magic is one of the simplest methods. Yet even in its seeming simplicity, there is a depth of magical knowledge one must possess in order for the spell to be successful. Just lighting a candle is not enough.

The universe itself is basically energy. Through scientific study, we know that matter consists of particles in motion at atomic and subatomic levels that our senses can't detect. If all things are energy, including us, then one can take the next step into a metaphysical realm and see how all things can be connected and intertwined on many levels. This energy vibrates at different speeds and there are varying levels of density. Practitioners of magic believe that this is one of the paths to making magic work—tapping into this great energy field by way of visualization. Everything we create begins with a thought.

Visualization

An important part of the process of raising energy toward a goal is visualization. This is how the energy knows what your goal is. More than just thinking of your goal or speaking it aloud, you must "see" it clearly in your mind as though it were real. Many practitioners consider the act of visualization to be the truest form of magic.

Visualization is the act of experiencing something vividly in your mind—seeing every detail as though it were right in front of you. Yet it's more than just seeing or imagining. Practicing this technique depends on specifics—sight, sound, colors, texture, taste, scent, and so on. A useful way to start is by imagining a piece of fruit, such as an orange or lemon. Close your eyes and try to imagine every detail of the fruit—hold it in your hand, see its color and texture, feel its weight.

Then imagine peeling it—the way it smells, the juice seeping out, the zest beneath your fingernails. Picture as much detail as you can. Can you taste it? Are you salivating?

Visualization is important not only for your magical intent, but it's also important when you're creating sacred space. We can visualize the energy we raise streaming out from our hands or from an object, such as a wand, carrying our goals and desires to the universe. You need to do more than just imagine the outcome of your spell—you must believe in it.

Intent: Your Magical Mind

As you can see, magic is more than words or objects, since these things do not contain power of their own. The power is within you, in your mind. Tools help us focus, but always remember the magic is you. I have a phrase I use to remind myself of this fact: it's called "The Power of ME." The ME stands for "My Energy" or "My Essence." This is your personal power.

Being able to focus your intent is the key to magic. Without that skill, raising all the energy in the world won't help you with your goal. This technique takes practice, but it's not complicated.

If you meditate, or even daydream a lot, you already have some understanding of the alpha state. These are the brainwaves produced when your mind is deeply relaxed. Visualization can be part of the alpha state as well. Slowing down the brainwaves results in deep sleep and trance—the theta state. These altered states of consciousness are where magic is made. When you work magic, your mind must be relaxed and, at the same time, focused on your goal. Your mind will be clear of everything else and you'll hold your visualized goal in your mind like a light.

Practicing meditation is a good way to learn how to clear your mind and reach a deep alpha state. There are many techniques for practicing meditation, and I urge you to explore them and find what works best for you. Here is one way to begin:

Sit in an upright position on the floor, using pillows if necessary. Sit in a chair if you need support for your back. Avoid lying down—this could cause you to fall asleep; even though you do want to be relaxed, you still want to keep your mind alert. Be sure your surroundings are quiet and that you won't be disturbed. Turn off your phone and any other noise or distractions. Breathe deeply in and out, trying to keep the breaths even. Count if you need to, such as breathing in to the count of four, and out to the count of four. Breathe through your nose. You can focus on an object if it helps you, such as a crystal or flower, but closing your eyes is recommended. The object is to clear your mind completely. Random thoughts will come to you, but gently dismiss them. Focus on your breathing. This is harder than it sounds. Try to remain in this state for five minutes the first time, then try for ten, fifteen, and twenty. Work your way up each day.

Music, especially drumming, can also induce this state. In addition, some say the music of Bach also has this effect. You may wish to play music that invokes a trancelike state when you are practicing candle magic.

Spells and Rituals: The Difference

Before we progress further, it's useful to understand the differences between rituals and spells. A ritual is a ceremony marking a special event or occasion, time of year, or rite of passage. Rituals can involve magic, but they don't have to. Some rituals act out a myth or are intended as a celebration, giving thanks, offerings, or honoring deity.

Spells are often done in a ritual or ceremonial setting, but not always. A spell is a call for change, an action toward a goal, or a positive affirmation or prayer. Spells are much like recipes—you can use existing ones and change them a bit to suit your needs, or create your own from scratch. A spell can be an elaborate magical working or a chant uttered on the spot when you need it. It can even be as simple as lighting a candle with focused intent.

Both of these workings usually involve creating sacred space. Without first creating sacred space, a ritual can become just meaningless action. Without sacred space for a spell, it may be more difficult for the practitioner to focus and achieve the state of mind that creates magic. Naturally, the more you practice, the easier it becomes to cast a spell without any tools or special preparation, but I still believe strongly that creating sacred space is important—it expresses a sense of reverence that improves your work. The more effort you put into it, the greater the meaning and the deeper your connection with the Divine. That said, in certain cases magic on the fly can be effective, especially in stressful situations where you don't have time or a place to prepare. Sometimes you feel a need so great that just your will alone is enough. This is especially true if you suffer from anxiety or deal with stressful situations—calling on your inner strength and power can help you stay calm and grounded, give you courage, and center you during difficult times. One could argue this really isn't a spell or magic, but I believe any working with your personal power and energy is a form of magic.

Making change in your life involves a kind of healing—magic helps with this by teaching you how to love yourself and remove negativity from your life, making room for acceptance. Self-examination is an important part of magical practice, and your spells will be more effective if you keep a positive attitude. This is not always easy—we all face difficulties from time to time in our lives.

Do Spells Really Work? How?

The act of carrying out a ritual or spell can be the magic itself—sometimes the act is more than the intended result. Think of it like an affirmation, in a big way. It's a focus, making a statement to your subconscious and to the universe of your intention and carrying it out physically, both magically and in the mundane world as well. Magic is a practice of interacting and engaging with energy and the Divine, however you perceive it. The altered state is like hypnosis. You are programming your mind with a thought so it can manifest, and you're asking the universe to act in accordance with your thought. This creates awareness and alignment with your goal, similar to the power of suggestion.

The way it works depends on whom you ask. Some practitioners claim that magic has a basis in quantum theory or some other scientific principle. Some say it's based on faith, and others claim to have no idea why their spells work. All admit that it's never certain and that the intent and state of mind are of utmost importance, whether alone or with a group. Magic helps a person work through challenges and focus on solutions.

The Magic Circle

Witches and other practitioners of magic have various ways of working. Nearly all of them involve the tradition of casting a circle. These are the preparations usually made before any ritual or spell is performed. It's a way to focus the mind and prepare for the act of magic. Casting a circle is not required, but it does help.

Magic can be spontaneous. It can also be well planned. Both ways work because the mind and intent of the user are the most powerful ingredients. However, most of us can use a little help focusing our mind on the mystical. We need to create a sacred space around us, especially if we're in an everyday place that seems ordinary. We need to make that place feel special, as though something amazing is going to happen there. We need to convince ourselves by setting up the space. And, for the spiritually minded, it's like going to a church or temple. Casting a magic circle (also simply referred to as "circle") is one way to do this, and it's really quite simple. It's about imagination and visualization, which we discussed earlier in this chapter.

Circles have long been considered to have a magical significance. In fact, circles have appeared in the art of cultures all over the world since the earliest people existed, from the Neolithic circles depicted on cave walls to the intricate mandalas of the East, in architecture, jewelry, and landscaping. Most candles you will create have a circle at the top and bottom. Our world is a circle—the Earth, sun, and moon are spheres. Patterns and cycles appear to be circular—it's no wonder the circle is such a powerful symbol! It is symbolic of life itself.

The purpose of the magic circle most likely originated in ceremonial magic as a means of protecting the magician against the powers of spirits he or she was trying to control. The circle of contemporary Wiccans and Witches is a bit different—it is intended to unite the practitioner with the forces of nature but not with intent to control those forces. The magic circle is said to be a place "between the worlds." One purpose it serves is to contain the raised energy until it is ready to be released. It also keeps out unwanted influences while the practitioner is working. The circle is a place of respect, and any natural forces or deities the practitioner invites to witness the ritual are asked, never commanded. Magic circles can be envisioned as moving with the practitioner, if necessary, and are usually considered to be more like spheres than just a circle on the ground. In addition, circles can be visualized to fill a room or encompass an entire house if needed. A limited space for your circle is easier to visualize, so start small if you're a beginner.

The circle is a visualization of your personal power, rising from you and creating a sphere around you. It can be marked with physical items to help you focus—you may stand or sit within an actual circle drawn of chalk or salt, for example, or a ring of stones or shells. The most common marker for magic circles is simply a set of four candles to mark each of the four directions, also called the four quarters. Picture a square within a circle. It's interesting to note that the circle is often considered to represent the self (the psyche), and the square of the four quarters represents the tangible earth.

Creating sacred space begins with the practical act of simply cleaning the area and organizing your tools and supplies. I like to play music while I do this, to set the mood. This is a good time to begin focusing your intent and getting into a magical state of mind. Set up your work area so that you'll have everything you need at hand. Wiccans and Witches often use an altar, which can be an elaborate table reserved only for magical use, or simply your kitchen table or other work surface. It becomes a special place when you visualize sacred space around you.

For those who may be unfamiliar with circle casting, I'll describe the process briefly. Eventually you'll find a method that works for you and appeals to your personal taste. A detailed outline is offered in Appendix B.

Usually the circle begins with creating sacred space, as we just discussed. This can involve more than just setting up and cleaning the area—it can also include a spiritual cleansing, often referred to as smudging. This is done by burning incense, such as sage, or sprinkling salt water around the area. The choice is yours.

The next step is to use visual markers at the four cardinal points (quarters) of the area that will contain your circle. Usually this step is done as part of the ritual, by the practitioner paying homage to those four cardinal directions or quarters (north, south, east, and west) and welcoming the four classical elements that they represent (earth, fire, air, and water, respectively). The four elements will be discussed in detail in Chapter 5. You can use white candles or appropriately colored ones if you have them:

North/Earth/Green

South/Fire/Red

East/Air/Yellow

West/Water/Blue

You can also use a symbol to represent each element, if you choose. For example, a stone for north/earth, a shell or dish of water for west/water, a feather or smoldering incense for east/air, and a candle for south/fire. You can place your markers at various areas around the room or simply at the corresponding locations on your work surface. Choose the most convenient method for your work.

It is customary to invite deity to be present in the circle as well. Wiccans often ask for the blessing of the Goddess and the God. Use your own personal preference. After you call the quarters or simply mark the cardinal points and welcome deity, then you can begin to visualize your circle. Often it helps to walk around in a clockwise fashion a few times to imagine the circle forming. If you practice Wicca or are familiar with magical practice, you may already have some magical tools to work with, such as a wand or athame.

When you are finished and wish to close the circle, you will first thank the deity and elements for their presence. Then walk in a counterclockwise direction and announce that the circle is closed.

In most cases you'll be performing a ritual or spell in the magic circle. However, the process of candle making can take hours, and you can't physically remain in the circle that long. I recommend saving the circle casting for the moment before you begin to infuse the molten wax with energy and pour it, and possibly again when you actually light the candle to use it in a spell. You can visualize the circle large enough to contain your entire kitchen or work area if you wish.

Candle Making as Ritual

The act of focusing meaning into action is all a ritual really is. It's symbolic, which is important to remember, since your state of mind while creating your candles is what gives them your own brand of power. The act of making the candle becomes a spell when you focus intent. While you're stirring the wax, adding the ingredients, pouring, visualizing your goal, or repeating your chant—keep your attention focused and your mind relaxed and clear of everything except your purpose.

Don't worry about giving the wax your undivided attention while it's melting. Go about your business in the house, but don't go very far—keep an eye on it and monitor the melting progress. I like to keep soothing music playing or incense burning in the room where the wax is melting. This way the sacred space is maintained, even if I leave the room. But the moment I return to the room, I refocus. The music and incense helps with this transition. I also like to wear a special ring on my projective hand (the one I stir and pour with) that helps me focus.

If you have a special place in your home you can dedicate to crafts and hobbies, consider yourself lucky. I have tried to use our basement or garage, but it seems like I always end up in the kitchen when making candles. This way, while the wax is melting, I can busy myself with other household tasks and still be near the stove.

Begin your spell when the wax is melted and reaches pouring temperature (see Chapter 1). The wax will be molten and free of any previous energy it may have collected. It's raw and ready—the wax is literally and figuratively ready to be molded by you.

You can cast your circle now, if desired. If not, simply begin your spell by stirring the wax very slowly. For all the spells and recipes in this book, the basic steps will be:

1. Add ingredients to melted wax
2. Stir, chant and visualize, focus your intent
3. Pour

The melted wax will wait for you. As long as the water stays hot, so will the wax. Just keep an eye on the temperature. You can keep the wax liquid for many hours with the burner on low—just make sure you keep water in the pot and continue to monitor the temperature.

Generally, a clockwise motion is used to increase energy and counterclockwise is used to dispel or decrease energy. This is the method that will be used throughout this book. In this case, you're starting by clearing old energy from used wax.

Here's a general chant to clear used wax of old energy. Stir in a counterclockwise motion and repeat these lines three times:

Molten wax of candles spent
clear your previous intent.

Next, begin to stir in a clockwise motion and say these words. Use this chant anytime you add fresh ingredients to create a magical candle, or simply want to empower the wax with your energy:

Infuse with power, hold it fast
until it is released at last.
Await your charge, a future spell.
Be blessed, and all your tasks be well.
You hold a sacred energy
for good of all, so mote it be.

If you're using new wax, you may omit the first two-line chant. Simply start with the clockwise stirring and chant to infuse.

If you're creating a specific spell candle at this time, first clear the wax, then use the specific words that pertain to that spell instead of the last six lines of this chant.

After the wax has been poured, you may close your circle (if you cast one) and go about your business as usual. The sacred space, even if you didn't cast a circle, is preserved as long as you keep it that way. For me, that means continuing to have the music playing or incense burning in the room. Keep the space sacred until your candles are complete and in the final cooling phase.

The next time you need to focus your intent is when topping off the candles. This doesn't have to be the whole circle routine, but it's still good to have a magical frame of mind. You can say a simple chant if you want to, but just having a magical intent will be enough.

The Importance of Candle Color

Many people believe colors have an effect on the brain and that certain colors evoke particular feelings and moods. There's a general rule about which colors are appropriate for a particular magical need, but if orange makes you think of love because of a sunset you experienced with a significant other, go ahead and use it!

Generally speaking, here are the basic colors and some of their various correspondences:

WHITE: neutral, all-purpose, full moon energy, protection, purity, meditation

BLACK: banishment, breaking bad habits

RED: protection, passion, energy, courage, strength, sexuality, will

PINK: romance, love, friendship, harmony, emotions

ORANGE: success, commerce, motivation, courage, legal problems

YELLOW: mental skills, communication, self-confidence, charm, travel, health, success

GREEN: money, fertility, growth, abundance, health

DARK BLUE: dream magic, transformation, instinct, psychic awareness

LIGHT BLUE: beginnings, endurance, awareness, joy

PALE VIOLET: inspiration, divination

DARK PURPLE: authority, leadership, mastery, spirituality, wisdom, psychic awareness, curse-breaking

GRAY: neutrality, mystery, dimness, concealment, secrets

BROWN: home, domestic issues, animals, grounding

Some of the most difficult wax colors to obtain are black, blue, purple, and sometimes yellow and orange. I once tried to make a batch of black candles by starting with white wax and a few chips of black wax; I ended up with an ugly greenish-gray color. If you want to make black candles, start with a darker shade, such as brown or purple, and add black chips. Experiment by mixing colors. You may want to just buy black candles (stock up right after Halloween). Or, you may need to purchase concentrated candle dye from a craft store to achieve your desired color. These are available in small wax blocks.

Sometimes I just make various batches of colored candles and charge them with general intent, adding no spell ingredients. I once had the good fortune to receive some bright sapphire blue wax and I wasn't sure what I'd use the candles for, so I just charged the molten wax with general magical intent and tucked away the finished candles for a future need.

The Magic of Words and Sounds

Words have power. Of course, you can't utter a phrase and make someone disappear, but words convey meaning and intent. If you have heard the term "self-fulfilling prophecy," you know that what people think about themselves often comes true—someone with low self-esteem will not be successful, because they lack confidence. Perpetuating that belief about one's self inhibits growth. But have you ever noticed that if someone repeats something about you, you start to believe it? This can be positive or negative. Words of encouragement are good to hear, as they help us believe in ourselves; harsh words can wear us down and cause us to doubt ourselves. The power of words shouldn't be underestimated.

You'll notice that most of the chants in these spells and rituals are quite simple, short, and rhyming. There is a reason for this, and it's due to the way our mind works. For one thing, it's easier for us to remember phrases that rhyme—that's why songs and ballads throughout history usually employ a rhyming pattern of some kind. In the days when people had a mainly oral tradition of storytelling and passing on lore and history, people could remember things more easily if the words rhymed.

Rhyme and meter also have another kind of effect on us. Think of music and dancing. There's something about particular beats that induce an almost trance-like state. This is certainly true of drumming circles, and tribes still use these practices today. It's a way of entering an altered state of consciousness—a magical mind.

People once believed (and some still do) that a person could curse another person with mere words, because the person being cursed believed so strongly in those words that he or she made it come true. In subtle ways, this can happen. Of course, we can protect ourselves by being self-aware and denying or laughing off the negative words of others. But thoughts and words do have power—as much or as little as we give them. Like candles, words and sounds are another tool of magic.

Music can also be used for magical workings. You don't have to play an instrument, but if you do, you can find ways to add this talent to your magical practice. Listening to music can help you enter a spiritual state of mind, so do so if it works for you. Be sure to select music that is not distracting—try to find music that you don't always listen to for fun, perhaps something special that you'll come to associate with magic. Instrumental pieces that are used in yoga can work well, and there are CDs available just for the purpose of magical practice. Some even have chants you can sing along with. There are also meditation CDs, collections of tribal sounds of flute and drums, and recordings of nature sounds. Experiment to find music that works for you.

Types of Magical Candles

This book contains recipes for various types of candles—spell candles, candles to enhance personal mood, elemental candles, and celestial candles. However, there are nearly endless ways to use candles in magic. Spell candles can also be considered an offering to a particular deity. Other types of candles that some practitioners use are altar candles, typically a pair—one to represent the Goddess and one for the God. These are commonly used on Wiccan altars and are lit as part of the circle casting, in addition to the elemental marker candles (if used). These are not required, but if you choose to create them, you can check Appendix A for some correspondences to use in creating candles dedicated to a particular deity. Many Wiccans focus on a general god and goddess pair, feminine and masculine energy, or white or silver for the Goddess and gold or yellow for the God.

Charging Candles

Sometimes you make candles months before you plan to use them or you create general magical candles that are not focused with a specific goal. In this case, you'll want to "charge" the candle just prior to using it in a spell. Think of your general magical candle as a blank piece of paper. It's just waiting for you to give it purpose, to write something on it. You focus your intent and purpose on the candle to charge it with your goal. The following are some common techniques for charging a candle.

You can anoint or "dress" your candles with essential oil. Place a drop of the oil on your finger or a piece of cloth and trace it along the candle, starting in the middle and going upward, then starting in the middle and going downward. Focus on your goal as you do this. You may wish to dilute your essential oil in a carrier oil so it doesn't irritate your skin if you handle the candle later on.

Carving is another method that can be combined with charging. While your mind is focused, use a crystal point or toothpick to carve words or symbols into the wax. See Chapter 10 for suggested symbols.

Or you can simply hold your candle while visualizing your goal. Typically, hold the candle in your projective hand (your dominant hand, the one you write with). See the energy flowing through your arm, into your fingers, and into the candle. Imagine it glowing with your personal power and intent.

Magical Ethics

Intent and attitude are very important in the practice of magic. If you believe all things are divine, this includes plants, animals, rocks, and us. Remember to respect all things and the free will of those around you. Project a loving, grateful attitude in all things you do; what you project can affect others, even if you don't realize it. This is true of most of our actions in life. This is why Wiccans perform magic according to the Wiccan Rede, "for the good of all" and "harm none." You wouldn't want someone manipulating your life without your knowledge, so don't perform magic for anyone without their consent, even healing. Always ask permission before you send energy to someone or perform any action that involves another person. Ultimately, ethics teaches us to live as though we are one with each other.

Magic is neither inherently good nor evil. It's a neutral force, like energy. The user can control whether to use it for a helpful or harmful purpose. Many practitioners of magic believe the energy that is sent out will return to the user. Wiccans refer to this as the Rule of Three because they believe that what you do will come back to you multiplied three times. Basically, these ethical beliefs mean you shouldn't harm or manipulate someone else. Don't do a spell for someone without their permission. If you want to wish someone well, do so—with the caveat that it be for the good of all. We are not to judge what is right or wrong for others. In addition, we all have different notions of what is "meant to be" and our own ideas of "freedom of choice." Fate, destiny—we all have different ideas about what that means. No matter what your belief system, you wouldn't want to be manipulated, so don't do it to anyone else.

Know too that you must be careful what you wish for. You may think you want something and get it, only to discover it comes with a very high price in other ways than monetary. (Perhaps you want a fancy car like your favorite Uncle Jack's. You do a spell to obtain such a car, then dear Uncle Jack's health fails and he can no longer drive himself. You've got the car you wanted, but you're not happy, are you?) Try to avoid being selfish, but realize that you deserve abundance in your life. You deserve to be happy, but not at the expense of others. These are ethics each person must work out for themselves. And always be prepared for unexpected results—your wish or desire may not manifest in exactly the way you imagine!

Attitude of Gratitude

Remember: always work in a reverent state of mind. As soon as the process becomes rote or mechanical, it loses the spiritual spark of magic. Prepare yourself by taking a ritual bath, smudging, or meditating—whatever you need to do to achieve a magical state of mind. Perform each ritual with a sense of gratitude and thankfulness. Never make demands or insist on one specific result. Be open to possibilities and you may find that an unexpected result turns out to be the best outcome.

Using candles for magic is a very simple and practical way of releasing energy into the universe to help enrich your life. Any purpose, need, or goal can be worked toward in this manner, but don't forget that you must also act in the mundane world as well. Lighting a candle and wishing to find a new job won't work if you aren't out there job hunting and going on interviews. Magic is a way of reinforcing your intent and projecting what you desire. Many spiritual leaders and psychologists promote the power of positive thinking and attitude. Some say "you are what you think." If that's the case, positive affirmations, wishes, prayers, and spells are all powerful ways to help you tap into your own personal power to achieve your goals. This is why candle magic works.

There are many wonderful books available that delve into magic and the philosophy behind it—the more you study the better your magic will be. But always remember that magic is natural and not the ground-shaking, lightning-bolt, substance-altering special effects of Hollywood and fantasy tales. Meaningful magic enhances our lives practically and spiritually, working in concert with the world around us.

Believe in yourself and the power of your subconscious mind. That's where the power begins. You hold within yourself the spark of divinity.

3

Candle Spell Ingredients

What the eyes perceive in herbs or stones or trees is not yet a remedy; the eyes see only the dross.

—PARACELSUS

M ost of the ingredients used in the spells in this book are common enough that you will have them in your kitchen or garden, or be able to purchase them easily. The main components are essential oils, flowers, resins, wood, spices, herbs, and stones. The addition of these ingredients is intended to enhance the magical correspondences of the candle. These are natural items that have their own special properties, both scientific and metaphysical. Learning more about these items can help you expand your practice and enhance your magical workings. Since your intent is the most important ingredient, don't worry if you can't find a specific item. Often there are substitutions if an ingredient is not available.

A list of some of the most common stones, herbs, and essential oils can be found in Appendix A, along with other correspondences you may find useful. This chapter will discuss the categories of spell candle ingredients and how to use them in candle making. I have focused on key ingredients that will enable you to do just about any kind of magic.

Herbs and Spices

A good deal of magic is done in the kitchen, which shouldn't be surprising. The kitchen was the domain of the Wise Woman, who prepared potions and brews. Modern Witches still do this, but we're usually brewing herbal tea or cooking food to nourish our bodies, minds, and spirits. In addition, every Wise Woman usually had a garden for herbs and other magical plants.

Herbs are the most common ingredient in these spells, and they should be added in their dried form in small amounts. Usually a pinch of dried herbs or spice is added to the molten wax, but sometimes a spell will call for a sprinkling of herbs to be added inside the candleholder or placed outside of it. Each spell in this book contains specific directions. You can use dried herbs that can be found in the spice section of the grocery store, or grow your own herbs and dry them.

Essential Oils

Most craft stores sell artificial additives to be used as candle scent. These can be overpowering and should not be used in magical candles—synthetic fragrances may decrease the power and essence of the candle as a magical tool. Keep in mind that magical candles are not intended to be room-fresheners. You will most likely not be able to detect the aroma when you burn these candles. These spells require only pure essential oils, recommended for their particular magical properties. Essential oils are very different from craft-store candle fragrances. They are highly concentrated essences distilled from plants and flowers and they can be expensive, but there are many common varieties that are affordable. And since you'll only need a few drops, your bottle should last a long time. Please note that essential oils are highly concentrated and most of them should never be applied directly to the skin. Always follow the directions on the bottle. Consult an aromatherapy book for further details on specific oils.

There are three specific ways to use essential oils in magical candle crafting. First, some spells call for adding a few drops to the molten wax to utilize the magical energy of the oil. Another way to use essential oils, especially if the scent appeals to you, is to add it to your candle while it's burning. When a pool of melted wax forms around the base of the wick, simply add a couple drops of oil. Like an aromatherapy burner, the heat will release the scent. It will be subtle, but effective. The aroma will fade after a short time, and then you can add a few more drops. Never add more than a few drops at a time, and wait between adding them. The final way to utilize oils is to anoint a finished candle before burning it. Using your fingertip or a cloth, smear a drop or two of essential oil around the outside of the candle while visualizing your intent.

There are two main ways essential oils work with candle magic:

1. Via aromatherapy properties regarding inhalation of the scent and its effect on the brain—such as relaxation, energy, and so on; and

2. Through the magical or metaphysical properties of the oil, which may be different from the magical properties of the actual herb, flower, or resin the oil is derived from. The magical properties are drawn from centuries of folklore and use of the plant, resin, or oil. These properties may differ slightly from the aromatherapy uses, so it's important to follow the direction for each spell carefully. An oil may serve a different purpose when added to the molten wax or used to anoint (magical) than it does when added to the burning candle (aromatherapy).

Aromatherapy is a topic that fills many volumes, so I'll only touch on it briefly here. Basically, it has been proven that scents affect our brains due to our olfactory system, which still holds many mysteries for scientists. Our noses contain at least a thousand different kinds of specialized receptors compared with only four in the eye, which indicates how important the power of scent is to the human body. Our body has an immediate response to smells; scents have a direct route to the brain. For example, certain aromas stimulate the brain to produce chemicals, such as serotonin and dopamine, creating a feeling of relaxation. Various aromas create different feelings, and this is one reason that aromatherapy is so popular.

In addition, plants have properties beyond their chemical makeup that magical practitioners draw upon for spells and rituals—these are their metaphysical properties, which simply means "beyond physical." These are some of the qualities of herbs and oils used in spells. For example, most people who work with herbs for natural healing know that chamomile is mildly sedative and peppermint can soothe an upset stomach. But other magical properties of chamomile and mint come from folklore, the shape of the plant, and so on, and include not only the taste and texture, but also the aroma of the plant and the oil.

Beyond this, when using aromatherapy for magic, it's important to visualize your goal as you inhale the scent. Like any type of magical tool, aromatherapy must be filled with your intent in order to clarify the purpose. For example, let's say you're adding an aromatherapy component to your candle spell by putting some drops of oil in the wax. You must inhale the scent while you visualize your intent, not merely sniff the scent and think, "Gee, that smells good."

Aromas have been an important part of spirituality throughout history. Various scents of plant materials were used as incense. A pleasant aroma was believed to please the gods, and it also covered unpleasant odors (more prevalent before modern plumbing). The smoke of incense was believed to carry prayers to the gods. Aromas are often used in candles, but really just a few drops are needed if you wish to incorporate aromatherapy into your burning.

The properties of some ingredients may seem contradictory when you compare the herb to the essential oil of the same plant. This is not only because the plant characteristics are not always the same as the aroma, but also because there are differing opinions about some of the qualities.

There are many aspects to consider when selecting magical correspondences. For example, one person who wants to create a spell to draw money may focus on the correspondences of the earth element. Someone else may focus on a particular plant or aroma. There are herbs and oils associated with attracting money that correspond to the fire element. In addition, folklore practices and ceremonial magic both influence the craft that Wiccans and modern Witches practice. There is bound to be some difference in opinion regarding certain ingredients. If you are ever in doubt, use your instinct to make a decision. You will also notice that many herbs have properties that include a full spectrum of uses. This is because the same herb would have a different, use depending on the intent of the user and the method in which it was used (eating, burning, carrying, etc.). Plants have "personality," and plants that are used for similar purposes have different subtle energies. Sometimes it comes down to accessibility and personal preference.

I have cross-referenced several sources and also taken my own usage into consideration for the lists in Appendix A. Some information on folklore practices gives a sample of the ancient traditions, and the contemporary metaphysical properties associated with each ingredient are also included. Please note that some herbs and spices are not safe to consume internally, and you should never ingest essential oils.

Stones and Crystals

I use the word *crystal* here to refer to more than just the common image of a clear quartz point. In this case, *crystal* refers to any mineral that is composed of a symmetrical order of molecules (which creates the smooth face of crystals we're familiar with). No matter if the mineral specimen is in shards, chunks, plates, or any other shape—it still has a regular, internal molecular order. Minerals with the same chemical composition can appear in very different forms (diamond and graphite are both carbon, for example). Because of their molecular elegance, magical practitioners have come to regard crystals as a symbol of order and balance.

Like other magical tools, crystals provide a way to fine tune and focus magical intent. Some users believe crystals work with the subtle energy of the body, what some people call the aura, and that the energy vibrations of different types of crystals can affect the body in various ways. In magical practice, users can hold, wear, or even carry the stones in order to benefit from their energy. In addition, those metaphysical properties can boost the energy of spells and rituals.

Before using stones and crystals in magic, they should first be "cleansed" by running them under water and visualizing them being cleared of any previous energy they may have—especially if you purchased your stone. There are many ways to cleanse stones, but this method is the easiest. Then you can charge your stone for a specific purpose. Speak your intent out loud if that helps you focus.

In candle magic, stones can be placed inside the mold before the molten wax is poured. The result is a candle with a piece of stone in the bottom, enhancing the potency of the magic. The stone can be removed easily from the remaining wax after the candle has burned out. Stones can also be placed inside or outside of the candleholder while the candle is burning. Chapter 10 contains a variety of ways to combine these various ingredients to create special arrangements for your spells and rituals.

Other Ingredients

In these spells you will also see ingredients such as resins and wood. Resins are dried bits of tree sap that are often used in incense. These are commonly ground and burned over special charcoal or other burning mediums, or used to create stick and cone incense. You should be able to find these ingredients at metaphysical shops or online. Be sure your source is reliable and that you're buying real ingredients. Frankincense is the most common and one of the oldest incenses used for spiritual practice. Some of these spells use sandalwood powder. There are many different ranges of quality of sandalwood and some are quite costly. Just use the best kind you can comfortably afford.

I recommend finding an inexpensive mortar and pestle so you can grind your resins and herbs together. You can probably crush most of the herbs and other plant materials in your hands, but resins are more difficult.

A Note about Using Ingredients in Candles...

Just use a pinch or drop of the ingredients; they are not meant to scent the candle, they are only meant to infuse the wax with their energy. In fact, too many additives and ingredients may cause the candle to not burn at all or, worse yet, catch on fire! Do not add more than what is called for in the spell. Remember: timing and intent are the most important aspects of magic. Stock your magical cabinet with the items listed in Appendix A and you should be prepared for anything.

4

Timing: When to Create and Use Your Magical Candles

The only reason for time is so that everything doesn't happen at once.

—ALBERT EINSTEIN

The timing of magic is important, and the more in tune you can be with the various correspondences, the better. These are traditions that have evolved over time, and they are deeply intertwined with myth, the seasons, and cultural practices. They are designed to create the most harmonious effect possible, giving your spell a better chance of success. Big efforts take time, so don't expect immediate results. All we can do is try to work in harmony with our surroundings for the best possible outcome. Remember that your intent is your strongest tool. Remember too that the best and most successful magic is the kind you work for yourself, out of sincere need or to improve your well-being.

Phases of the Moon

Moon phases are important in many of the world's religions, including in the Muslim, Hebrew, Hindu, and Buddhist lunar calendars. Most Wiccans and modern Witches pay more attention to moon phase than any other magical correspondence; it's usually the first aspect considered when a spell is being planned. We work with phases of the moon due to the belief that the moon's energy influences our lives in many ways. This will be explored further in Chapter 7.

The general rules for timing according to moon phase are as follows:

WAXING TO FULL MOON: to draw something into your life, increase

FULL MOON: time of greatest magical power

WANING MOON PHASE TO DARK MOON: to reduce or eliminate something from your life

DARK MOON: contemplation, meditation, self-exploration

NEW MOON: beginnings, fresh starts

You may hear the terms "new moon" and "dark moon" used interchangeably, but there is an important distinction that needs to be recognized for magical practice. Astronomically, the new moon is considered to be the phase when the moon is not visible from Earth, thus, it is "dark." However, "new moon" originally meant the very first *visible* crescent moon. Magically speaking, we will distinguish between these phases and call the invisible moon "dark" and the very first visible crescent the "new moon." Some magicians approach it this way: the waning moon becomes "dark" when it is completely invisible and then it becomes "new" when it can be seen. Please note, however, that most calendars call the "invisible" moon the new moon. Some practitioners consider the dark moon to be the very final waning phase just before the astronomical moment of new moon, when the moon is aligned with the sun. Again, spells in this book consider the moon to be "dark" when it's invisible and "new" when you can see the first waxing crescent in the sky.

Most everyone is familiar with phrase "blue moon." We define this as the second full moon of a calendar month, but this definition actually came about by accident. In 1946, a writer for *Sky and Telescope* magazine used this definition due to a misinterpretation of the *Maine Farmers' Almanac*. The actual original definition was the occurrence of a third full moon in a season that had four full moons instead of the usual three. However, this "new" definition regarding months stuck around, and that's how we interpret "blue moon" today.

There is also a rare and lesser-known term called "black moon." This is not a commonly used astronomical term, but it has been used to occasionally refer to the following rare situations: when a new moon occurs twice in a calendar month (similar to our contemporary definition of a blue moon), or when four new moos appear in a season (similar to the original definition of a blue moon). Consult a lunar calendar to watch for these occurrences and perform magic if you wish. If you want exact calculations of the lunar phases, you can find lunar calendars and almanacs online or in stores, or check astronomy books and magazines for more information.

General and Defined Intent

There are two main ways to work with magical candles: create them with a specific purpose in mind, or create them with general magical intent to be charged later for a specific purpose. We'll call these categories defined intent and general intent.

Candles for a Specific Spell—Defined Intent

When you create a candle with a defined goal in mind, the creation of the candle is part of the spell. You'll want to have a chant or visualization prepared, or a specific goal to focus on while you're making the candle. This book provides spell "recipes" for candles intended for a specific purpose.

For these defined-use candles, you don't have to burn them immediately, but the point is that they're already charged with specific intent. For example, you can create an entire batch of prosperity candles and burn one each month during the waxing moon, if you desire.

When creating spell candles with specific intent, the timing can be very important. Let's say you want to create a candle to draw love into your life. You create the candle at the appropriate time, such as during a waxing moon phase. But you also want to burn the candle at an equally appropriate time to ensure success, so be sure to burn it before the moon wanes, or save it for the next cycle. For breaking a bad habit, create the candle during a waning or new moon and burn it during a waning moon phase.

Once you've created a specific spell candle, all you need to do to complete the spell is to light it to release the energy. However, you may need to refocus your intent before lighting it, simply to remind yourself of the purpose and goal. The reason for this is magical intent. Candles are tools, and the act of making them and performing a spell helps focus the mind, which is where the real magic resides. You can cast a circle and make the burning of your candle part of a ritual, or you can simply take a few moments to put yourself in a magical state of mind and revisualize your goal. Even though you charged the candle with energy when you created it, being in a magical state of mind when burning it is also important.

Candles for a Future Spell—General Intent

When you're making a batch of candles for future use in spells, it really doesn't matter when you make them—they will be infused with your personal energy and charged with specific purpose later. However, I try to select a day during a full moon to create my candles, just for the added magical influence.

I like to make general batches of candles in many different colors so I always have a variety on hand. I usually keep several of each color and lots of white ones for all-purpose use. Again, the time of the full moon is generally a good time to make candles, since it holds added magical power. But you can make most candles anytime, as long as you remember to burn them at the appropriate time for your spell. The only exception to this rule is when you're creating some of the celestial candles; these are designed to be created (as well as burned) during the appropriate moon phase. We will further explore celestial candles in Chapter 7.

———————

Timing involves more than the moon phase; other aspects to consider include the day of the week, the moon sign, time of day, and so on. Details are provided with each spell in this book and in Appendix A. You can use as many levels of correspondences as you wish, depending on your current need.

If you must make your candles at a different time than you plan to burn them, just use the general spell to energize your wax (see page 36) and then charge the candles later for a specific spell before burning. Sometimes, due to convenience, we must make several batches of candles at once. I recommend making a general batch anytime of the year during a waxing or full moon phase. Use an appropriate chant later to charge the candle for its specific purpose. Or, let's say you want to make a batch of pink candles but are not sure yet what you'll use them for. Just use the general chant on page 36 to infuse them with energy.

Sometimes I want to set aside an entire day to make candles. Obviously, this can't always accommodate every type of spell or sabbat candle. As I mentioned previously, you can charge your candles with general intent and save them for future use.

Here's one example: On a Friday during a waxing moon, I made a batch of green prosperity candles to be used throughout the year. I followed the recipe beginning on page 147 and will chant and visualize my goal again when I light the candles. In addition, since it was also a good day for love candles, I made some for renewing romance (see pages 140–143). Since I had all my candle-making equipment out, I went ahead and made some general gray and white candles to be used in the future. And, because it was a sunny day, I made some sun candles even though it was a Friday (not a Sunday). I charged them in sunlight, and then charged them again the following Sunday. I plan to use these in the future by charging them for healing or success. Since the moon was in Aries that day, I made some red protection candles as well.

As you can see, it's fine to take advantage of whatever time you have to make candles and create a variety at one time. When you're ready to use the candles in a spell, charge them for the specific purpose—use the details provided in each spell recipe for chants and information on other correspondences. The more correspondences you can take advantage of, the more it enhances your work.

Correspondences for Days of the Week

Monday

Ruled by the moon, Monday is a good day to work with emotions, cycles, feminine issues, birth, inspiration, travel, needs and desires, divination, and balance. This is a good day for spells that involve family, domestic issues, dreams, nurturing, meditation, and psychic abilities.

COLOR: white and silver, along with other iridescent colors and pastel shades
SCENTS: sandalwood, lemon, jasmine, gardenia
STONES/METALS: clear or milky quartz, pearl moonstone
PLANTS: willow, chamomile, mushrooms, banana, cucumber, lotus
ELEMENT AND SIGN: water, Cancer

Tuesday

Tuesday gets its name from Tiu or Tiw, an Anglo-Saxon god that is comparable to the Roman god Mars, god of war. Magic for Tuesday includes action, initiation, leadership, courage, protection, strength, passion, energy, and politics.

COLORS: red
SCENTS: ginger, pine, pepper
STONES/METALS: bloodstone, garnet, ruby, iron
PLANTS: basil, garlic, ginger, radish, holly tree
ELEMENT AND SIGN: fire, Aries

Wednesday

This day is named for the Norse god Woden or Odin, the Roman counterpart of Mercury, the messenger god. This is a good day for magic involving communication, writing, networking, mental skills, creativity, memory, and business.

COLORS: violet, yellow
SCENTS: benzoin, eucalyptus, lavender
STONES/METALS: opal, agate, citrine quartz
PLANTS: caraway, dill, fennel, lavender, parsley, trees of ash or hazel
ELEMENT AND SIGN: air or water, Gemini or Virgo

Thursday

This day is ruled by Jupiter and named for the Norse thunder god, Thor. This is a good day for magic involving growth or expansion of any kind, in addition to learning, good fortune, wisdom, wealth, honor, responsibility, spirituality, philosophy, religion, and law. But use caution: sometimes you can get more than you expect.

COLORS: purple, royal blue
SCENTS: clove, star anise, nutmeg, cedar
STONES/METALS: amethyst, turquoise
PLANTS: oak trees, anise, clover, dandelion, juniper, mint, mistletoe, sage
ELEMENT AND SIGN: air or fire, Sagittarius

Friday

Friday is Freya's day, a Norse goddess similar to the Roman Venus, the goddess of love. Forms of magic to use on this day are those for beauty, love, romance, abundance, harmony, friendship, fertility, and pleasure.

COLORS: green, pink
SCENTS: rose, yarrow, almond, vanilla
STONES/METALS: rose quartz, emerald, amber
PLANTS: apple, aloe, rose, geranium, mint, raspberry, thyme, violet
ELEMENT AND SIGN: earth or water, Taurus or Libra

Saturday

This day is named for the Roman god Saturn, god of agriculture. We know him as the figure of Father Time. Magic for today includes spells for structure, self-discipline, change, order, removing obstacles, and binding.

COLORS: black, dark blue, brown
SCENTS: myrrh, patchouli, copal, cypress
STONES/METALS: onyx, sapphire, hematite, obsidian, tiger's eye, lead
PLANTS: beets, hemp, mandrake, thyme, pomegranate
ELEMENT AND SIGN: water or earth, Capricorn

Sunday

Sunday is, of course, named for the sun. Magic for this day includes success, self-empowerment, confidence, health, leadership ability, aspirations, pride, and power.

COLORS: gold, yellow

SCENTS: frankincense, rosemary, cinnamon, cedar

STONES/METALS: gold, pyrite (for its gold luster), amber, diamond, tiger's eye

PLANTS: citrus fruits, sunflower, marigold, rosemary, St. John's Wort, birch and laurel trees

ELEMENT AND SIGN: fire, Leo

Moon phase is probably the most important correspondence; color is also important. Day of the week should be considered if possible during candle creation, but in my opinion, day of the week is more important for burning time. The days of the week have been constructed by our society's calendar and—while the names of the days have celestial significance and the influence can be present—I believe it is a secondary consideration to the moon phase and wax color. The type of element and energy is also important and should be one of the primary considerations. In addition, the moon sign is another correspondence to include, if desired. Combine as many correspondences and associations as you can. Magic will typically follow the path of least resistance, so work with your current situation. If you have time to plan ahead, that's great, but often we have a need that doesn't fit the current day or moon phase. In that case, use color and elemental energy as your focus; or you might consider numerology or aroma. Enhance your intent the best way you are able.

The spells and recipes in this book are already set up to include the proper correspondences for each purpose. You can use the timing information here to further enhance your spell or to create your own spell (see Chapter 10). For example, if you created some general intent candles and you decide you want to use one for a specific purpose, you would charge your candle and burn it according to these timing suggestions and the correspondences in Appendix A. You can be as creative as you like with the correspondences. Once you have chosen the appropriate day of the week and moon phase, select some of the items to use in your spell—burn incense, arrange stones or plants on your altar around your candle, and so on. You can even select a candleholder in one of the corresponding colors or use an appropriately colored cloth to cover your altar or table.

For example, say you made a batch of white candles with no particular intent, except that they will be used for magic. You decide to use one candle to increase prosperity and another to banish debt. Your goal and the time of burning will be different—one is to lose, the other to gain. To increase prosperity, burn on a waxing or full moon; to decrease debt, burn during the waning moon phase. You would also accompany each spell with other correspondences, such as herbs, stones, and so on, to heighten the magical impact.

Burning Methods

If you have studied magic or plan to read more about it, you will likely encounter a variety of "rules" for how to burn candles. Some will say to always use a match to light them, or to never blow out a candle (use a snuffer). Whatever you believe is the best method for your practice is what you should do. I see no reason why you can't light a candle with a regular lighter (although, like other magical tools, you may wish to designate one just for candle magic). I snuff candles sometimes simply because it's a nice method to put them out and you don't risk blowing hot wax everywhere. But sometimes I do just blow them out. One good tip is to place your hand on the opposite side of the flame so when you blow it out, you blow toward your hand—this also helps keep the wax from being blown off the top of the candle.

There are also many different opinions on how long to let a candle burn. Some spells specifically say you should allow the candle to burn out completely. Depending on your situation and time constraints, this is not always possible. (This is one reason it's a good idea to make half-size paper cup votive candles—they burn out more quickly than larger candles.) If you cannot attend your candle until it burns itself out, it's perfectly fine to put out the flame and light it again later. This could continue for several days. Some spells are even written this way intentionally, planning for your candle to burn for a few hours every day for a specific period of time. And, if your candle goes out immediately after you light it, perhaps the wick is too short. Try to light it again. If that doesn't work, try a different candle.

Candles made from recycled wax may not always burn evenly, and they may also appear to have burned out but still have a tiny flame. Always be sure a candle is extinguished if you plan to leave the area or go to sleep.

When the Candle Burns Out

After a spell candle has burned out, I often leave it on the altar or table until I feel the spell has manifested, or until I simply sense that it's time to remove it. This can be a day, several days, or a week. This is completely up to you.

After your candle spell is completed, you have a few options, depending on the type of candle. If you had herbs or resins in the wax, you may have to simply throw away the spent wax. If the wax is clean, and in a large piece, feel free to reuse it if you can—melting it will remove any of its previous magical energy. It's usually best to discard very small wax pieces.

You should always discard plant materials you used in a spell, such as plants you used to lay on the altar around the candle. Just leave them outside as an offering to the Earth. Stones should be cleansed (often by simply rinsing with water) so they can be reused.

Always remember to burn candles safely! Use a glass or other type of heatproof container for your candles. Another method is to use a plate or tray, but be sure that any running wax will not spill. A large glass plate or tray is a nice way to surround your candles with herbs, plants, flowers, stones, and other items. You may still want to put your candles in containers, though, unless you don't mind the wax running into the items. Sometimes I do this with herbs and stones. After the puddle of wax cools, I can simply remove the stones and discard the spent wax and the herbs imbedded in it. Sometimes I can reuse the candle, because I sprinkled the herbs on the plate instead of putting them in the candle. Some spells actually call for the wax to spill over onto an object or piece of paper that will be disposed of when the spell is complete.

Most of the time, especially if you're using a plate or large glass container, the candle will simply pop out of a container after it has cooled. If you have difficulty removing a spent candle, try this technique. In the bathroom or kitchen, fill the sink with the hottest tap water possible. As you're running the water, put the candle container in the basin and allow the water to fill it up and completely cover it. Allow this to sit for a few minutes, but not too long or the wax will cool again. Carefully, while the water is still warm, use a fork or knife to pull the wax free from the container. The hot water that surrounds the container and fills it should soften the wax considerably. A common kitchen knife is always useful to remove wax—just be careful not to cut yourself or break any glass.

5

Elemental Candles

One touch of nature makes the whole world kin.

—WILLIAM SHAKESPEARE

This chapter discusses creating candles specifically to be used as elemental markers during a ritual. In addition, these candles can be used in a spell that corresponds to a particular element—for example, an earth candle for a money spell or an air candle for help in retaining knowledge.

What Are the Four Elements?

In many magical traditions, practitioners use a representation of each of the classical elements during circles created for rituals and spells. This is useful in marking the directions of north, south, east, and west (often referred to as the quarters), but it also serves a higher purpose: to honor the four elements that make life possible. We would not be here without soil to live on and the land to nourish us, the heat and energy of the sun to warm us and create food, the oxygen we breathe, and the water we drink. This is what makes these elements so special. They are all connected, intertwined with us and our lives.

In Wiccan traditions, the pentagram, or five-pointed star, is considered a representation of the four elements plus Spirit, which is also considered by some to be an element. The actual five-pointed star is called the pentagram; when it's enclosed in a circle, it's referred to as a pentacle. Each point of the star represents an element, with the outer circle symbolizing that all things are connected. In addition, the pentacle as an object (often made of wood, stone, or clay) is often used to symbolize the element of earth on Wiccan altars. This symbol has a rich history, and many traditions have ascribed various meanings to it. Despite the variety in its use, it has almost always been associated with magic and is often considered to be a protective talisman. The number five is common in nature, and five-pointed stars are found in nearly every culture—in ancient Egypt, Greece, and Rome, and even in early Christian cultures. They're mostly decorative, but the use of the pentagram in Western magic probably originated in the twelfth century. Some of this is based on the human body—we have five senses and five fingers or toes on each limb—and spread out the body makes a star. The pentacle is often associated with Solomon, a Christian magician. It was mentioned in the tale of *Sir Gawain and the Green Knight* and is considered a divine form and endless knot. But probably what firmly fixed it as a magical symbol is a famous sixteenth-century European book on magic, Cornelius Agrippa's *De Occulta Philosophia*, in which pentagrams were depicted as being used in a Magic Circle.

Please note that Wiccans do not associate the pentacle or pentagram in any way with Satan, which is a construct of Christianity. Wiccans do not believe in Satan or in any other supreme evil being. Some traditions use the symbol with the top point of the star pointed down; this too can have various meanings, depending on one's tradition. In Wicca, it is almost exclusively used with the top point of the star pointing up.

Spirit
white

Air
yellow

Water
blue

Earth
green

Fire
red

The correspondences for the days of the week given in Chapter 4 include some information about what element is governed by a certain planetary influence. However, there are more details to learn about elemental correspondences.

Air (east) is the element that rules mental skills, intuition, psychic ability, communication, consciousness, creative ideas, study, travel, freedom, and knowledge. Symbols for air include feathers, birds (and other feathered creatures, both real and mythical), clouds, circles, eggs, incense smoke, and flowers. Music associated with air includes sounds produced by flutes, bells, pipes, and other wind instruments. Senses connected to the air element are hearing and smell. Places are windy places, mountain tops, and the sky. Air is nearly always connected with spiritual practice because many cultures believe the divine ones live in the sky and that's the direction prayers are sent. Some believe the smoke of incense can carry prayers to the Divine. Air is a projective energy, meaning that it's a good way to send thoughts and energy out into the universe. When you think of air, consider the very air that we breathe, but also think of wind, the atmosphere, and the sky. Magical tools associated with air are the wand, staff, broom, and incense burner. Air is considered to have masculine energy. Its signs of the zodiac are Gemini, Libra, and Aquarius. Some scents that stimulate the qualities of the air element are mint, dill, lavender, lemongrass, parsley, pine, sage, and star anise. In the Tarot, air corresponds to the suit of Swords.

Fire (south) is the element that rules energy, cleansing, sex, passion, protection, courage, strength, banishing negativity, and transformation. Symbols for fire include flames, the sun, and the triangle. Music associated with the fire element contains the sound of string instruments. The sense of sight is associated with fire. Places include ovens, hearths, deserts, and volcanoes. Fire is a projective energy, like air, and is good for magic that creates change. Think of the way fire transforms things—it is destructive, but also creative. A forest fire is devastating, yet there are some plant seeds that can only be awakened by fire, and fire also clears the way for a fresh start. Fire also changed the way humans live—discovering fire enabled us to cook food that we would normally not be able to eat. In addition, think of stars in connection with fire, as our sun is a star. Without that heat and light, we would not have the life on Earth that we know. Magical tools for fire are the sword, athame (ritual knife), and the incense burner (this item is associated with both fire and air, for obvious reasons). Fire and air depend on each other because fire can't exist without oxygen to feed it, and, like air, fire is considered masculine energy. Its signs of the zodiac are Aries, Leo, and Sagittarius. Some aromas associated with the element of fire are basil, clove, copal, frankincense, ginger, orange, and rosemary. In the Tarot, fire corresponds to the suit of Wands.

Water (west) is the element that rules purification, healing, emotions, nurturing, rejuvenation, sleep and dreams, love and friendship, peace, psychic awareness, intuition, feelings, the unconscious mind, mysteries, and birth. Symbols for water include shells, the cauldron or other types of cups and vessels, the upside-down triangle, and any type of water. Music associated with the water element includes sounds made by rattles, cymbals, and bells. The sense associated with water is taste. Places are areas where water exists—springs, wells, oceans, rivers, lakes, ponds, and so on. Water is a receptive energy, meaning that it's good for drawing things to you, and it's considered to be feminine energy. Remember when thinking of water to consider things like fog, mist, ice, and snow. Mirrors are also associated with water magic. Bathing and ritual cleansing are types of water magic as well. Water is used as a cleansing element in this way in many cultures. Think of the act of baptism, a kind of spiritual rebirth. Salt water is considered to be protective. Magical tools associated with water are the chalice (ritual cup) and cauldron. Its signs of the zodiac are Cancer, Scorpio, and Pisces. Some scents that evoke qualities of the water element are apple, chamomile, freesia, gardenia, geranium, hyacinth, iris, jasmine, lily, mugwort, myrrh, rose, sandalwood, thyme, vanilla, yarrow, and ylang-ylang. In the Tarot, water corresponds to the suit of Cups.

Earth (north) is the element that rules all things mundane and domestic. Like water, it's a nurturing energy, but it's also stabilizing and governs money, prosperity, grounding, employment, the body, health, love, and gardening. Symbols for the earth element include the square, the cornucopia, wheat and acorns, soil, leaves, and stones. Music for the earth element includes drums and all percussion. The sense associated with earth is touch. Places are caves, mountains, woods, gardens, fertile fields, and circles of standing stones (like Stonehenge). Earth is a receptive and feminine energy, like water, so it's good for manifestation and drawing things to you. Knot magic and binding are other forms of earth magic. Earth governs the cycles of death and rebirth—just think of the four seasons in nature and the life cycles of all living things. The magical tool associated with earth is the pentacle. Cauldrons are also associated with earth since, like water, earth is symbolic of life cycles and rebirth. Think of Mother Earth, our home. We live on the land and return to it. We eat what the earth provides, but that wouldn't be possible without the other elements as well. That's one reason the pentacle symbol represents earth—because we wouldn't even be alive without the nourishment provided by this complex and miraculous combination of elements. Its signs of the zodiac are Taurus, Virgo, and Capricorn. Some aromas associated with the earth element are cypress, honeysuckle, lilac, oakmoss, patchouli, tulip, and vetivert. In the Tarot, earth corresponds to the suit of Pentacles.

In many ways, all the elements depend on each other. Notice, too, that the projective and receptive elements have many similarities—air and fire, earth and water. All the elements have destructive powers as well (earthquakes, floods, fires, and tornadoes). Remember this and have respect for these awesome forces of nature.

The Fifth Element

So what exactly is that element represented by the top point of the pentagram? It can have many definitions. Some call it Spirit, the Center, the source of all things, the life force itself. Others simply call it God or Goddess, the representation of the Divine in all forms. It is all things and yet nothing. While some pentacles with color correspondences show this point as purple or pink, other color associations are the neutral colors: clear, white, or black. The spirit represents transcendence, the turning of the Wheel of the Year, and the wheel of life. Beyond time and space, all is one. If you would like to create a candle or candles to represent Spirit, use white wax or any color that appeals to you. Visualize whatever you like—this is a very individual and personal element for most of us. Write your own chant or prayer; make or burn this candle anytime you like.

Combining the Elements

These four elements shape the world we live in and have caused our planet to change dramatically over millions of years. Obviously, since our existence and world is made up of the relationship between these four classical elements, they work together in magic as they do in nature. Many of the spells in this book combine correspondences of two (or more) elements. That's because all things are connected and specific needs often span more than one element.

Consider personal transformation, one of the most beneficial forms of magic. Fire is an element of transformation, but its energy style is projective. Most people think of self-transformation as receptive energy, and in most ways it is. But in this case, combining the transformative energy of fire with a receptive energy like water or earth is the ideal magic. And since this is candle magic, fire is automatically present, providing the transformational quality of change that is at the root of all magic. Adding correspondences of water or earth would give the spell a receptive quality.

Working with the Elements: Calling the Quarters

Traditional basic correspondences:

North/earth/green

South/fire/red

East/air/yellow

West/water/blue

If you don't have the appropriate colored wax, use white and burn the candle in a colored glass container.

The goal for these candles is to create the candle and charge it with the specific element as you create it. Candles are traditionally used to represent fire, but you can still create a candle specifically for any element by empowering it using other correspondences. There are many ways to accent each of the elemental properties—there are various herbs and oils that can be associated with each element; adding a few to each candle reinforces the power of that element.

Several options will be given for each elemental candle. You don't have to follow all of them. Choose the one(s) that will work best for you. For example, if you can't create the air candles at dawn, that's all right; choose an appropriate day of the week. If that's not possible, choose a time with the appropriate moon or sun sign. If you'd like to plan in advance, spend a year creating your elemental candles during their corresponding season. The object is to give you as many creative options as possible. Suggested herbs, resins, and oils are mentioned in each recipe, but feel free to experiment with other associations as you desire. Consult reference books and use your imagination.

Your elemental candles can be used as more than quarter candles in a magic circle. They are useful for spells that correspond to the various properties of each element. Remember: you don't have to follow all the suggestions listed, just choose one or two (or more) that you like.

Elemental correspondences are an integral part of magic and, obviously, the element of fire is a major component in candle magic. But the elements of earth, air, and water can be incorporated in various ways. It's also important to understand that the obvious elemental properties of stones and herbs merely scratch the surface of their application. Plants may seem an easy choice for the element of earth, and they can certainly be used that way, but each plant has an elemental and planetary association, like a personality. The same goes for stones. They, too, can represent the earth element in a spell, but each one has a personality that can correspond with a different element. These personalities are based on folklore and both scientific and metaphysical properties.

Elemental Earth Candle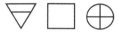

The wax for this candle should be stirred in a clockwise motion while facing north. You may also listen to percussive music, lots of drums and rhythm, while creating the candle.

TIMING: Create this candle when the sun or moon is in an earth sign— Taurus, Virgo, or Capricorn; on a Friday (ruled by Venus) or Saturday (ruled by Saturn); late in the evening if possible, midnight is best; or during winter.

INGREDIENTS: A pinch of dried oak leaves and one drop of patchouli oil.

OTHER OPTIONS: Place a small quartz crystal (or any stone) at the bottom of the candle mold; place a pentacle symbol in the bottom of the mold, such as a pendant; carve a pentacle symbol into the hardened candle.

Speak the chant four times just after you add the ingredients.

EARTH ELEMENT CHANT: *Field, forest, flower, stone,*
Earth that is our fertile home,
Lend this wax your energy—
As I will so mote it be.

Elemental Air Candle

Face east while stirring the wax for this candle in a clockwise motion. You may choose to burn incense while creating the candles and wave some of the smoke near the molten wax, allow a breeze to blow in through an open window, or visualize wind and the sky, movement of air. You can also carve elemental symbols into the finished candle. Try listening to music of flutes and other wind instruments while creating these candles.

TIMING: Create this candle when the sun or moon is in an air sign—Gemini, Libra, or Aquarius; on a Wednesday (ruled by Mercury) or Thursday (ruled by Jupiter); in the morning, at dawn if possible; or during spring.

INGREDIENTS: A pinch of dried lavender and one drop of peppermint oil.

Speak the chant four times just after you add the ingredients.

AIR ELEMENT CHANT: *Air that moves us, air we breathe,*
Give this wax your energy.
Wind or gale, as you please,
Flow into it like a breeze.

Elemental Fire Candle

Face south while stirring the wax for this candle in a clockwise motion, focusing on passion, strength, transformation, or protective qualities and energy. Visualize fire, the sun, or anything you associate with this element. You might also carve an elemental symbol or the sun into the finished candle. Listen to music of string instruments while creating the candles.

> **TIMING:** Create this candle when the sun or moon is in a fire sign—Aries, Leo, or Sagittarius; on a Sunday (ruled by the sun) or Tuesday (ruled by Mars); during midday; or in summer.

> **INGREDIENTS:** A pinch of dried basil or rosemary, a pinch of ground dragon's blood resin or frankincense resin, and a pinch of ground ginger powder.

Speak the chant four times just after you add the ingredients.

FIRE ELEMENT CHANT: *Spark to flame,*
Create, ignite,
candle, candle burning bright—
Lend this wax your strength and light.

Elemental Water Candle ▽ ⊖

Face west while stirring the wax in a clockwise motion. Visualize forms of water such as rivers, waterfalls, springs, lakes, the ocean, rain, or even snow—whatever image(s) appeals to you. Listen to music containing rattles, cymbals, and bells, or ring a bell over the molten wax. Place a tiny sea shell in the mold, or carve elemental water symbol into finished candle.

TIMING: Create this candle when the sun or moon is in a water sign—Cancer, Pisces, or Scorpio; on a Monday (ruled by the moon); in the evening, at twilight if possible; or during autumn.

INGREDIENTS: A pinch of dried fern, willow, water lily, or gardenia; one dried rose petal or three drops of rose oil; and a pinch of dried myrrh resin or sandalwood powder.

Speak the chant four times just after you add the ingredients.

WATER ELEMENT CHANT: *Rain and river,*
Ocean, stream,
Water, water,
Wash us clean.

Anoint finished candle by dipping it into water (allow it to dry before burning).

Calling the Quarters

Here is a chant you can use to call the quarters when you cast a circle. As you welcome each element, light the appropriate candle.

I greet the North
and honor the element of Earth.
Sand and soil I call home,
field, flower, tree and stone.
May the earth nourish me.

I greet the East
and honor the element of Air.
Changing winds, air to breathe,
precious atmosphere and breeze.
May the air inspire me.

I greet the South
and honor the element of Fire.
Energy of sun so bright,
Warmth and heat, radiant light.
May the fire excite me.

I greet the West
and honor the element of Water.
Drink of life in flow or freeze,
Rain and river, spring and sea.
May the water renew me.

Earth, air, fire, water—all unite to make a whole;
body, mind, heart, and blood—build the world and the soul.

6 | Sabbat Candles

We see the flowers fade and the leaves fall; but we likewise see fruits ripen, and new buds shoot forth. Life belongs to the living; and he who lives must be prepared for vicissitudes.

—JOHANN WOLFGANG VON GOETHE

This book corresponds to seasons in the Northern Hemisphere. If you reside in the Southern Hemisphere, please make the appropriate adjustments.

The Wheel of the Year

We often think of time in a linear fashion, moving from a beginning to an end, marking time by our modern calendar. But in temperate climates, seasons repeat in a cycle that feels more circular. The wheel turns, and the seasons mirror the cycles of our lives. In nature we see birth, death, and rebirth. Time and life are often depicted by symbols of spirals and wheels turning, spinning around and around.

The word *sabbat* has obscure origins but most likely comes from the Hebrew *Shabbath*, which means "sacred" or "holy." Wiccans use it as a term for the eight major holidays they celebrate throughout the year. You will also see the word *esbat* used in Wiccan practice. Esbats (or ebats) take place on the full moon and this word comes from the French *s'ébattre*, which means "to have a good time" or "to frolic." This word may also be used to designate other special times when Wiccans celebrate alone or in groups, or gather for a ritual or to work magic.

Those who practice Wicca or other Neo-Pagan paths will already be familiar with the seasonal celebrations described here. I offer this information because whether you are new to this path or not, it is relevant to making the connections that are important for the sabbat candles.

The Old Ways

This calendar we call the Wheel of the Year is loosely based on the Pagan practices of the ancient Irish and Celts. The Celts were a tribal people who lived in Europe during the Iron Age, in parts of the British Isles and areas that are today France and parts of Italy and Switzerland (northwest Europe). The name comes from the Greeks, who called them *Keltoi*. Much of what we know about them, since they had an oral tradition, comes from the writings of the Romans, and much of this lore has been lost. We do know that the most important celebrations appear to have been the festivals of Samhain, Beltane, Imbolc, and Lughnasadh, when entire tribes would gather for ritual, prayer, feasting, and socializing. In addition, the solstices were also acknowledged. Other European cultures have influenced this Wheel of the Year as well, including the Romans and the Germanic people of northern Europe, the Norse. They had some similar myths, festivals, and practices. These ancient peoples had a sophisticated method of plotting the course of the moon and sun, and it is by way of the old customs that many of our modern holidays have evolved. Much of the lore of these people has been lost over the ages, so we know very little for certain, only what historians and anthropologists have been able to piece together based on artifacts and some writings that were penned long after the ancient peoples lived.

If you imagine this calendar as a wheel with eight spokes, with Winter Solstice at the top, there are four quarter days and four cross-quarter days. The quarter days—Imbolc, Beltane, Lughnasadh, and Samhain—fall between the solstices and equinoxes and were believed to be particularly powerful times of the year. These days marked thresholds of time when there were visible changes in the natural seasons. Each quarter was considered a gateway, and each period contained a cycle of rest, sprouting, and bearing fruit, related to their pastoral and agricultural ways of life. In addition, it's useful to note the relevance of Samhain and Beltane, as these times marked a transition between the dark and light halves of the year. In fact, the times of Samhain and Beltane were thought to be spirit nights—mysterious and magical times when the doorway between realms was accessible. This was potentially dangerous, and yet aroused curiosity and superstition.

The solstices and equinoxes, which we refer to as the cross-quarter days, are times that can be measured by placement of the sun. The solstices were of primary importance. On the solstices, the sun appears to rise and set in the same place for a few days—it appears to be standing still. That's what the word *solstice* means—it comes from the Latin *sol stetit*, "the sun stood still." We know these times as Winter Solstice, the longest night, and Summer Solstice, the longest day. The ancients followed the path of the sun in the sky throughout the year and noticed changes; namely, that the sun appeared to move in an arc. The sun would have appeared high overhead during the summer, but lower in the sky in the winter. The solstices were boundary times occurring at the halfway point of the dark and light halves of the year. Even though we mark the Winter Solstice as the first day of winter and the Summer Solstice as the first day of summer on our modern calendar, to the Celtic people these would have been midwinter and midsummer.

Equinox means "equal night"—a time of balance and change, renewal and harvest, when day and night are equal in length. We know these as times that mark the first day of spring and the first day of autumn on our modern calendar. While it has not been documented that these ancient tribes actually held festivals on the equinoxes, they were able to recognize these patterns of time.

Obviously the dates that we use in our modern calendar would not have been the exact time of these sabbat celebrations—there is no way our calendar today could be equated exactly with the times these people lived. One important difference is that the Celts placed a great deal of emphasis on the moon, and their days are believed to have begun at sunset. In addition, the seasonal festivals may have been celebrated on the full moon during that time. For example, Samhain celebrations would have occurred on the first full moon of the winter season (our calendar month of November) and not necessarily on October 31. This is just the date our calendar marks as Halloween, the modern evolution of this ancient festival. The Celtic calendar was more flexible than the calendar we know today.

So what does this have to do with candles? Well, for one thing, many magical practitioners are Wiccan or follow other paths of Pagan spirituality, so they identify with these traditions and seek various ways to honor them. Not surprisingly, fire was a major way to celebrate just about any public gathering. Fire is symbolic of power, and it was believed by many cultures to be a gift from the gods. Even though we're mainly focusing on the Celtic and Norse myths here, you can find similar traditions in other cultures.

Since many of the people of ancient Europe settled in the United States, many Americans have ancestors who may have been part of Celtic, Norse, or other European cultures. This makes these celebrations relevant to Wiccans. In addition, the North American climate and seasons are very similar to those in Britain, where the Celts lived, so the cycles match what many Americans experience (save the extreme northern and southern areas, perhaps).

Even if you don't specifically follow the path of Wicca, ultimately these celebrations are based on the seasonal cycles of nature and they can be easily incorporated into any spiritual path. You'll notice that most of these holidays somehow concern the movement of light, due to the influence of the sun. Since candles represent light, they are the perfect symbol for the changing light in our lives. Whatever your spiritual path, celebrating the seasons can be a meaningful experience. The goal is to integrate what we know from the past into celebrations for today.

It's important to note that no pre-Christian people celebrated all eight of these days—this Wheel of the Year is a collection of traditions that we can use as a structure with our modern calendar to celebrate the seasons and cycles of nature. We are not trying to reconstruct ancient practices; rather, we are drawing on seasonal celebrations that people have honored throughout the ages, borrowing some of their traditions and influence, and adding our own personal touches in order to honor the seasonal significance and make these days relevant to our lives.

A General Rule for Sabbat Candles

One of the best parts about making many votives from one batch of wax is that you will have finished candles you can use within a day and some to save for the future. Depending on how much wax you use and how large you make your candles, you can make up to a dozen at a time. These candles will be infused with the influences of the season they are created in, but, since there wasn't an exact date for most of these ancient festivals, as long as you make them within a week or ten days of the sabbat, it's close enough. This way, you can use them for your celebration on that particular day if you desire. In fact, festival days traditionally lasted three days before and three days after the designated day. Or, you can make these candles on the sabbat as part of your ritual. You can even do this as a group, and everyone can have a candle to use for their personal celebrations or spells. When making candles for a solstice or equinox, remember that since the actual moment of solstice or equinox can be determined using an almanac, you may want to try creating a batch at that precise time.

Just because a candle was created with a sabbat influence doesn't mean you can only burn it for that purpose. Save these candles to use throughout the year for rekindling a particular mood or enhancing a specific spell. Suggestions for this are given with each recipe.

And remember: unless the recipe specifically calls for an item to be added to the mold, only use a pinch of the herbal/resin blend for the entire batch of wax. Too many additives can ruin the candles and pose a fire risk. Use dried herbs in tiny pieces—crumble them between your fingers, use a mortar and pestle, or buy them already ground.

The chants given here should be used while stirring the molten wax just after adding any necessary ingredients.

Winter Solstice—Return of the Light

The Winter Solstice (sometimes referred to as Yule) is the shortest day and the longest night of the year. This is the time of year that many cultures around the world celebrate the "return of the sun," since after today the days gradually lengthen, the light increases, and hope for the next growing season is renewed. The solstice usually falls on or around December 21. In the depths of winter, this time marked a change in the sun's movement and the increased light meant the winter season was at its halfway point. Candles are the perfect symbol for this celebration of light, as are sun symbols and spirals, which represent eternal life.

The origin of the word *Yule* is a topic of some debate, but the Winter Solstice was a major feast, especially among the Scandinavian and Norse peoples. It was a festival of revelry that lasted for weeks.

WAX COLOR: Red and green are traditional colors often associated with decorations for this holiday; however, since the Winter Solstice is a solar festival, you can also use yellow or gold wax.

TIMING: Create the candles a day or two in advance, night or day; at the time of sunrise on the day of the solstice; or at the exact moment of solstice in your time zone (as determined by consulting an almanac). Consider using them for an evening ritual, or light them at sunrise to welcome the light. See the Suggestions for Ritual section for more ideas.

INGREDIENTS: A pinch each of ground frankincense, ground cloves, and cinnamon and three drops of juniper oil. Frankincense, cinnamon, and cloves are associated with spirituality and the element of fire. In addition, these scents often evoke a celebratory and spiritual frame of mind. Juniper oil is also associated with the element of fire and the sun, as is frankincense.

Mix the resin, cloves, and cinnamon in a mortar and pestle and grind to a very fine powder. Add just a small pinch of this mixture to the molten wax, and burn the rest as incense while you work. Add three drops of juniper oil to the molten wax just prior to pouring.

YULE CHANT: *Welcome Sun, returning light,*
Give us solace from the night.
Linger long throughout the days,
Bless us with your glowing rays.

Drawing on the work of authors such as Sir James Frazer (*The Golden Bough*), Wiccan authors and other folklorists have constructed the speculative myth of the Holly King and Oak King. This is based on a collection of myths and stories from various cultures, representing the changing seasons and folklore associated with trees, which were sacred to the Celts. The main idea behind this myth is the symbolic battle between dark and light, though it's actually more like a changing of the guard. At Winter Solstice, the Oak King takes over to lead the land through the time of growing light; at the Summer Solstice, the Holly King takes control during the darkening half of the year. They are dual aspects of the masculine personification of nature. Here's a poem you may wish to incorporate into your solstice ritual.

A Villanelle for the Winter Solstice

Once again the light has come
to bring us longer days.
Welcome Thee, midwinter sun,
bringing warmth to everyone
in many joyous ways.
Once again the light has come,
the Holly King, his time is done,
upon the ground he lays.
Welcome Thee, midwinter sun.
Oak King now his battle won,
light the Yuletide blaze.
Once again the light has come,
reign of sunlight has begun,
with cheer our cups we raise.
Welcome Thee, midwinter sun,
darkness is at last undone,
we sing a song of praise.
Once again the light has come,
welcome Thee, midwinter sun.

SUGGESTIONS FOR RITUAL

Incorporate seasonal decorations such as evergreens and star symbols into your celebration. Remember, the sun is a star. The star symbol that many people think of as biblical this time of year has many other, older associations.

This holiday, more than any other, is a celebration of light and of the sun. Arrange several candles in the shape of a five-pointed star on your altar or table. You can use your hand-made candles as the five points, and fill in the connecting lines with small white tea lights if you wish. Or, burn your candles in holders decorated with stars.

Wishing spells are common solstice magic. Typically, a person writes a wish on a piece of paper and then burns it. You can light these with the flame of your hand-made candles, then allow the paper to burn safely, or carve your wish into the candle and allow it to burn completely. Some people like to stay up all night to greet the sun and allow their candle to burn as they keep vigil, encouraging the return of the light, as our ancestors may have done.

Imbolc—Life Stirs

Even though the land is cold, warmth is stirring. Life begins to come forth from the depths of winter. This was considered by the inhabitants of ancient Britain to be the beginning of the spring quarter of the year, which includes our months of February, March, and April.

This celebration was called Imbolc (or Imbolg) and we celebrate it around February 1. Some say that the word *imbolg* is related to the Celtic word for milk, since this was the start of the lambing season. Rituals for this holiday honor Brigit (Brigid), Celtic goddess of healing, smithcraft, and poetry—fire is one of her symbols, and she is associated with creative inspiration.

The sun is gaining strength. In addition, the roots of our modern Groundhog Day come from this time of year, when divination practices were popular. During this time of year, when winter still seems to reign despite the lengthening days, people were anxious about the future and eager to hear predictions. This time during the yearly cycle is a time for transformation, moving from inner contemplation to outward manifestation.

WAX COLOR: White or pale green.

TIMING: Create these candles on February 1 or 2—or in advance for use in your Imbolc celebration. This is a nurturing time,and can be a good time to initiate a project, especially a creative one. Make candles at Imbolc to give to new mothers or to anyone who has (or could use more) nurturing qualities. Visualize a nurturing quality as you prepare these candles. Play soft music and imagine nature awakening.

INGREDIENTS: Add a pinch of ground sandalwood and three drops of chamomile essential oil to the wax. Both chamomile oil and sandalwood have feminine energy. Both ingredients induce a calming effect.

You can use all your candles in a ritual or save some Imbolc candles to use anytime you need nurturing, want to boost your creative spirit, or need to feel a sense of renewal.

A Chant for Brigit

Warm me, Brigit, light the fire,
Within and without.
In transformation and desire,
Extinguish all my doubt.
Teach me, Brigit, light the flame,
My passions burning higher.
Creative spark I seek to claim —
Let me be inspired.
Heal me, Brigit, hearth ignite,
Help me know the way.
Guide me with your sacred light,
With me always stay.

SUGGESTIONS FOR RITUAL

Make a large batch of these in small sizes in order to have an abundance of light. Make a circle with your candles on a white plate or mirror. Ask for the blessing of Brigit or for any of the qualities she possesses—inspiration, nurturing, renewal, or purification. Frost your candles with white wax to give the appearance of snow (see Chapter 10 for details).

Spring Equinox—Rebirth

The Vernal Equinox marks a time when day and night are equal in length, so balance is often celebrated now. And, of course, the first day of spring is a time to celebrate the rebirth of the land. Most cultures and religions have some kind of spring holiday structured around a birth or resurrection story to honor the cycle of birth, death, and rebirth. The Christian Easter holiday occurs around this time of year—the Sunday after the first full moon after the equinox.

The word *Easter* may come from a German goddess called Eostre, a goddess of spring. The other possible source is the Anglo-Saxon word *eastre*, which is associated with the season of spring, opening, and new beginnings. No matter the source, this is astronomically the time of the equinox, and so it deserves some attention as the first official day of spring. Wiccans refer to this day as Ostara. This day usually falls somewhere around March 21.

WAX COLOR: White.

TIMING: Make these candles a few days before the equinox and use them for your ritual that day, or make them on the equinox and use them in a future spell for balance, renewal, a seed blessing (see Beltane spell for similar ideas), or healing.

INGREDIENTS: Two drops of either ginger, orange, or pine (or a combination) to promote physical energy. Place a tiny piece of egg shell or a seed in the bottom of the mold. Since it may float, push the item to the bottom of the mold (using one of the wicks with a metal tab attached) when the wax begins to thicken.

As you create these candles, visualize rebirth of some kind—this could be spiritual or literally the rebirth of nature after winter.

A Rebirthing Chant: *Spring draws near, bud to flower,*
Light increases by the hour.
Balance comes to day and night,
Candles represent the light.

SUGGESTIONS FOR RITUAL

Decorate your altar with the symbols of the season. Try the simple approach—tiny buds that haven't opened yet or delicate flowers that are blooming at this time in your area, such as crocus, daffodil, and tulip. This is a time of awakening—some places in warm areas are nearing full bloom; others still have snow on the ground.

Beltane—Fertility and Protection

Beltane is a time to celebrate the abundance and fertility of the spring season in full bloom: life, love, growth, and sexuality. Part of the name Beltane (or Beltaine) comes from the old Celtic word *tene*, which refers to fire, but the origins of the rest of the name are uncertain. It could mean "brilliant" or "lucky fire," or refer to Belenos, a Celtic sun god similar to the Roman Apollo. Whatever the meaning, people did celebrate with fire. One custom involved jumping over a bonfire. Leaping between two fires was said to bring good fortune. Again, fire is an important symbol, and candles are a perfect way to represent this.

Celebrated in North America on May 1, Beltane is believed to be one of the major Celtic festivals, ushering in the summer quarter, which includes our months of May, June, and July.

WAX COLOR: Red or white.

TIMING: Make these candles on Beltane or May Eve (April 30) and use them to empower a future magical working for fertility, love, romance, or any type of growth or abundance that you seek. Alternately, make candles just prior to the sabbat and burn them on Beltane as part of your ritual.

INGREDIENTS: A pinch of dried thyme, ruled by Venus (goddess of love); a pinch of dried basil for fertility; and a pinch of dried rosemary to represent the Maiden.

BELTANE CHANT: *Lush and fertile grows the land,*
Mother Earth please guide my hand.
Field, forest, flower, tree—
Abundant blessings come from thee.

The pinch of herbs should be enough for several candles. As you pour, visualize the aspects of Beltane that you wish to evoke. Are you working on a project that you want to bring to fruition? Do you seek to celebrate love or increase love in your life? Pour your intent with the molten wax.

SUGGESTIONS FOR RITUAL

This is also a good time for garden blessings and protection rituals, since it's time to begin planting in many areas. Use these candles in a seed-blessing ritual or a ritual to prepare the land. For a seed-blessing ritual, place your seeds (or seedling plants) in the center of your altar and surround them with candles. Be careful if using plants—keep them clear of the flames. Visualize the energy from the candles flowing into the seeds or plants, filling them with vitality and strength. To bless the land, scoop up a small amount of garden soil and place it in the center of the circle. Bless the soil, and then return it to the garden. Visualize it filled with energy to help your plants grow strong. Make a batch of red candles and a batch of white candles for a lovely display of contrasts. Decorate with red and white roses or make a mini maypole and circle it with candles.

If you have a garden, keep in mind that gardening is similar to making homemade candles—growing your own herbs, flowers, and vegetables infuses them with personal power. These can make potent magical ingredients for your spells.

Midsummer—Summer Solstice

This is the height of the growing season—the Summer Solstice, or Midsummer, the midpoint of the Celtic summer season. Occurring around June 21, this is the longest day and the shortest night of the year. Wiccans sometimes call it Litha, a nontraditional name that is possibly of Saxon origin. This festival was popular among the early Germanic peoples. The sun is at its strongest point today, yet beginning at this moment, the darkness begins to gain as the nights gradually grow longer. Again, as at Beltane, the ancients celebrated with fire. The festival often began the previous night, on Midsummer Eve, and there are many legends and tales of faeries and other forest folk that frolic in the mysterious and lush summer woodlands. This night was thought to be one of the most magical nights of the year.

WAX COLOR: Green or white.

TIMING: Create these candles on Midsummer or Midsummer Eve and use them for any future magical working—it will add a boost to your power. Or, simply make them prior to the sabbat and burn them on that day as part of your ritual.

INGREDIENTS: Two drops of rosemary essential oil to represent feminine energy of the Maiden and a pinch of dried mint leaves. Mint has a long history of being used in magic.

Returning to the Holly King and Oak King myth, here is a poem to recite as you visualize your candles being filled with magic:

A SONNET FOR THE SUMMER SOLSTICE
The land is soaked in light of longest day,
The leaves of all the trees invoke a spell—
The night will bring the frolic of the fae
And music of a foxglove's graceful bell.

The potent plants—verbena, rose, and rue;
The mythic battle that this day evokes;
A turning of the Wheel as ever true:
The Holly King defeats the King of Oaks.

Upon the night the moon is poised to shine,
Her silver touch turns grass to burnished blades.
The woods are lush with lichen, herb, and vine,
While winged magic dances in the glades.

We now begin the waning of the year—
We welcome this Midsummer night with cheer!

SUGGESTIONS FOR RITUAL

If you can, have a bonfire party—make wishes and dance. Celebrate life! To-night is a good night for magic of any kind. Use your candles to decorate for an outdoor event. If you made them on the solstice day, burn them for any type of spell, especially those that require solar energy. Decorate your altar with a dish of water and make floating candles by using a mini-muffin tin as a mold. Decorate your altar with seasonal flowers.

Lughnasadh—First Fruits

On or around August 1, we celebrate the festival of Lughnasadh (loo-nuh-suh). In Ireland this is known as "the assembly of Lugh," and it's the first of the three harvest months—our months of August, September, and October. Lugh, often called "the many-skilled," was a god similar to the Roman Mercury—he was fast, intelligent, and a guardian of travelers. People celebrated with games and feasting and, to honor the beginning of the harvest, breads were baked. The Anglo-Saxons celebrated a feast day called "hlaef-mass" or "loaf-mass," which came to be called Lammas. At this time, a loaf of bread made from the first grain was ritually blessed at the altar. This is a good time to look back at what has been sown throughout the year and begin to reap rewards; at the same time, look ahead and plan for next year.

WAX COLOR: Orange or yellow.

TIMING: Make these candles prior to your celebration or ritual, or make them on this day for a future spell involving confidence, goals, and success. While Lugh isn't exactly a sun god (although he is sometimes associated with the sun), he is "many-skilled," and this competent influence can be used for any goal you are pursuing.

INGREDIENTS: A pinch of dried sage for longevity and wisdom; a pinch of dried chamomile flowers, associated with masculine energy; and four drops of lavender oil, ruled by Mercury.

A Harvesting Chant:	*Sickle, scythe sever sheaves,*
	fruit and grain, stems and leaves.
	Light is low, bless the bread,
	taste first fruits—we are fed.
Or:	*The wheel has turned and once again,*
	the seasons circle without end.
	We reap now what we've sown this year:
	some fruit to keep and land to clear.
	Water, wind, soil, and sun—
	Harvest season has begun.

Visualize mastery for whatever you need. Consider your goals and the skills you need to succeed. Imagine your goals achieved, your dreams coming true. This is the time to focus on self-confidence. You are reaping what you've sown and seeing the rewards of time invested in hard work and effort.

SUGGESTIONS FOR RITUAL

Just prior to the main harvest celebration in September, we begin to prepare by assessing what we have sown and what we still need to nurture. This is also a good time to celebrate your accomplishments and talents. Be proud of what you have done this year and think about future plans—what will you sow next?

Bake a special loaf of bread today and, if you made your candles in advance, burn them in your kitchen while you work. Bake loaves of bread for gifts as home blessings and give candles with them.

Autumn Equinox—Harvest

The Autumnal Equinox usually falls around September 21. Although fall officially begins this month according to our modern calendar, in ancient Britain this was the midpoint of the autumn season.

Sometimes Wiccans call this celebration Mabon, for the Welsh god Maponos or Mabon ap Mordron, who was a youthful figure, lover, and musician, also known as a great hunter in some legends. He came to be equated with Apollo by the Romans.

At this time of the year, the sun moves into the astrological sign of Libra, represented by the scales, symbolic of balance.

WAX COLOR: Brown or yellow.

TIMING: Make these candles prior to your harvest celebration and use them that day in your ritual or spell, or create candles on the day of the equinox to use in a future spell for balance or abundance.

INGREDIENTS: A pinch of dried and crushed oak leaf for good luck, and four drops of patchouli or vetivert oil (these oils have an earthy aroma).

BALANCING CHANT:

Change is in the air,
Yet balance rules the day.
Change is in the air,
And if it comes my way,
I will balance all,
Be stronger, come what may.

As you stir, chant, visualize, and ask for balance in your life. Or, if you need change, focus on that. Give thanks for the harvest season. Save some of these candles for a Thanksgiving celebration.

SUGGESTIONS FOR RITUAL
Celebrate the harvest by creating a special feast. Use your candle as part of a centerpiece or altar decoration. This candle looks particularly rustic and perfect for the harvest home when "frosted" or encrusted with spices (see Chapter 10). Create a spell for harvesting whatever you need to in your life. This simply means reaping the rewards of something you started—a project of any kind. Decorate with pumpkins, gourds, acorns, leaves, and other seasonal items.

Samhain—Summer's End

Samhain (sow-ihn, *sow* is pronounced like *cow*) was one of the most important times of the Celtic year. The word *samhain* means "summer's end." This time of year marks the beginning of the winter quarter—our months of November, December, and January. In the seventh century, the Christians set aside November 1 as All Saints' Day, also known as Hallowmas or Hollantide. So, the night before came to be known as All Hallows Eve, and eventually was shortened to Halloween. It's the end of October, a mysterious time when the world seems to be dying, but nature is actually getting ready for a time of repose. This is naturally a time when people ponder death and wonder about the spirit world. And, as for many other Celtic festivals, sacred fires were lit on hilltops to ward off unwelcome spirits; a modern custom uses candles in windows to guide departed spirits on their way.

This is a time of year to confront one's fears of change and death. As this was considered to be one of the three spirit nights, Samhain was also reputed to be a popular night for divination. This is a threshold, a borderline, a time of change and transformation.

Samhain candles may be used as simple decoration for your home or for your special ritual. The occasion is both somber and joyous, a time of darkness and new beginnings. On the night when the spirit world is near, these candles will light the way for any who need guidance. They will empower your ritual with the sacred elements of the night.

WAX COLOR: Black or red.

TIMING: You can create these candles on Samhain morning for use later that night, or make them a day or two ahead. You can even make extra and save them for next year; they will still hold their power. Or, make creating these candles part of your evening ritual and burn them on Samhain the following year or as part of other spells and rituals when you wish to evoke this special season.

INGREDIENTS: A pinch of dried parsley to guide spirits, three drops of cedar oil for purification, and a pinch of ground myrrh resin to evoke feelings of spirituality.

SAMHAIN CHANT: *At summer's end, embrace the night,*
A candle's flame within our sight.
Guiding spirits as they roam,
Near to us or far from home.
Guide us, too, who walk the Earth,
Bring our journey love and mirth.
Until we slip beyond the veil,
And those who follow tell our tale.

SUGGESTIONS FOR RITUAL

Place one or more of these candles in windows to guide the spirits (use caution with curtains) or use them in Jack-o-Lanterns. Carve them with celestial symbols. You can also use these candles on an altar decorated with seasonal items, such as gourds, apples, leaves, and nuts. Or, make an altar dedicated to the memory of your ancestors or other departed loved ones and light one of these candles for them.

————————

I invite you to explore and study the deep and rich history surrounding festivals, myths, and folklore of a variety of cultures, but understand that seasonal celebrations are timeless. Ultimately, observing your surroundings and creating your own rituals is the most rewarding practice.

7 | Celestial Candles

Remember that you are this universe and that this universe is you.

—JOY HARJO

Gazing up at the night sky, we feel a sense of awe and mystery. Modern science has revealed that we are truly children of the stars: the various elements of life were formed in these giant gas clouds. In addition, the sun and moon govern our lives in many ways. Ancient peoples who worshipped the sun as a god knew what they were doing—truly this celestial sphere can take part of the credit as our creator. The gas cloud that formed our star also spawned the planets, with Earth forming in just the right place to sustain human life. It's amazing to consider how everything came together to bring us to where we are today.

And consider the mystical moon. The most widely accepted theory of the creation of the moon is that an object impacted Earth during its early formation stage. The impact of this object, the debris of which formed our moon, caused Earth to tilt, resulting in our seasonal changes, weather patterns, and climate. The moon stabilizes this tilt and the climate, which is vital to the evolution of life as we know it.

So when humans of long ago gazed up to the sky, worshipping those heavenly bodies—sun, moon, stars, and planets—they weren't too far off in their assessment that these objects were important to our lives, maybe even sacred. In fact, they are responsible for our very existence! If one tiny thing had been different, maybe none of us would be here. Call it divine influence or fortunate accident; either way, it's astonishing and miraculous.

In Wiccan practices, the sun and moon are often symbols of the Divine, the sun representing the masculine half and the moon as the feminine. Both have a long history of being associated with various forms of magic.

Refer to Chapter 4 for more details about timing for these spells. For maximum results, try to make these celestial candles at the suggested time. Add the appropriate ingredients and speak the included chant aloud while you stir the molten wax, just before pouring into molds.

Lunar and Solar Candles

Why make lunar or solar candles? This is an excellent way to fine-tune specific spells. Let's say you want to do some solstice magic, either summer or winter. The solstice is a solar festival, based on the position of the sun. So you may want to use candles that have been charged with sunlight for extra energy in your solstice spell or ritual.

Or maybe you want to do some spells associated with issues ruled by the moon (dreams, emotions, inspiration, meditation, psychic work, etc.) or a specific moon goddess. Lunar candles would be appropriate for this type of work.

You can use the correspondences for days of the week in Chapter 4 to get more suggestions on planetary correspondences. You may also refer to Appendix A. For now, let's explore the influences of the sun and moon.

The Moon

As you probably know, the moon moves through a cycle of phases approximately every 29½ days. Due to the movement of the moon around Earth and the amount of sunlight shining on it, the moon appears to grow and shrink, wax and wane, and we see the moon change from crescent to full and back again to crescent. In addition, the moon, like the sun, moves through the constellations of the zodiac. This is what we mean when we say the moon is in a particular sign. It takes the sun a year to move through the signs (you know this based on your birth sign), but the moon completes the twelve-sign journey in just over 27 days (if you study astrology, you probably know your natal moon sign as well). Everything from emotions, weather, health and bodily functions, and gardening can be studied with the phases of the moon in mind.

Maiden, Mother, and Crone

There is particular feminine symbolism associated with the phases of the moon: the Maiden, Mother, and Crone. The Maiden is youth personified, a young woman growing to adulthood. Sometimes she is depicted as a virgin. This is the new moon. The moon waxes and grows to the full moon: the Mother. She is the nurturing mother goddess, caring for all and filled with love and the ripeness of womanhood. The moon wanes as age progresses, and the Mother becomes the Crone, the elder Wise Woman, holding the knowledge of a long life and giving advice to those who seek it. Meditate on these images as you wish during the various phases of the moon. In Greek mythology, the three goddesses associated with this Triple Goddess aspect are Artemis (Maiden/waxing crescent), Selene (Mother/full moon), and Hecate (Crone/waning crescent). These aspects are a cycle that mirrors life—birth to adolescence, adulthood and prime of life, and old age to death of the body—these birth-death-rebirth cycles repeat over and over again.

Women are particularly in tune with cycles, as they experience the cycles of menstruation with a similar timing—approximately every 28–30 days the body waxes and wanes to prepare for possible birth. This is one reason women have often felt a special connection to the moon and why the moon is considered to have feminine qualities in many cultures. In fact, the word *menstruation* comes from the Latin *mensis*, which means "month" or "moon."

In magical workings, each phase has a particular significance. From the new moon to waxing crescent is considered to be a good time for introspection, growth, beginning new projects, making plans, making changes, renewal, and other personal endeavors. As the moon grows, this powerful energy expands and magical expression includes more high-energy actions: interaction with other people, making positive change, and other magic involving outward projection. The waning moon phase is a good time for banishing and breaking bad habits, and the dark moon is traditionally a time of intuition, reflection, meditation, and rest. The dark moon time can also be used as a period for healing and dreaming. The half-moons are called second quarter (waxing) and fourth quarter (waning). (The new moon is sometimes called the first quarter, and the full moon is called the third quarter.)

Further, there are thirteen lunar cycles each year. Since our calendar only has twelve months, one month will sometimes contain two full moons. This second one is called a "blue moon." Of course, the moon really isn't blue in color; this is a just a phrase, as discussed in Chapter 4. Ancient peoples often had names for the various full moons of each month, based on the seasons. Groups such as the Celts and the Native Americans gave names to these moons, which we still use today.

For example, the full moon closest to the Autumn Equinox is called the Harvest Moon. The assumption is that people could work in the fields by moonlight to bring in the harvest.

Generally speaking, you can work with your personal power or energy as it relates to the moon in a particular way. Think of this as internal, personal power expanding as the moon grows. In addition, moon phases mirror the cycles of life and the changing seasons—again, birth–death–rebirth.

The moon (along with the sun) affects Earth in other ways as well, namely the tides. And since the majority of the human body is made up of water, it's no wonder that we should feel the effects of the moon and seek to work with that energy.

Full Moon Candles

Creating a candle during the full moon is the most powerful time for magic. While this is a good time to create candles of any color for any purpose, this recipe is specifically for candles to be used to celebrate the full moon phase.

WAX COLOR: White.

TIMING: These candles should be created on the day or night of a full moon (or simply at night). Generally the day before and after the actual day of the full moon can also be considered full moon days.

INGREDIENTS: A pinch of sandalwood powder. Optional: a pinch of dried flowers such as gardenia or jasmine or a pinch of aloe leaf, or two drops jasmine essential oil or eucalyptus oil.

FULL MOON CHANT: *Magic moon please cast your light*
on these candles here tonight.
Infuse with energy and power,
grow in strength each passing hour.

Speak the chant twice.

Visualize white moonlight streaming down directly into the wax, filling it with power and magic. Pour your candles. If possible, allow the candles to sit outside overnight or beneath a window where moonlight can shine on them. If you'd like, place a tiny chip of moonstone in the bottom of the mold. Full moon candles are good to use for psychic power and abilities, fulfillment, and general celebration.

Dark Moon Candles

The time when the moon has waned to complete darkness, just before the new moon begins to grow, is a powerful and mysterious time. You can use black wax for these candles, but it may be difficult to find black wax to recycle. Look for colored wax additives at your local craft store. If you still can't obtain black wax, you may use white, since white is an all-purpose color. Mark white candles with a waning crescent moon symbol after they harden so you can remember these are for dark moon magic.

Avoid associating the word *dark* with evil or ill-intent. There is a balance in nature, yin and yang, forces that coexist in harmony and define each other. Dark is the necessary opposite of light and is considered to be symbolic of self-exploration and discovering the depths of one's soul. Many myths and stories speak of a hero enduring the darkness before emerging into the light, meaning there are challenges to be faced in order to achieve success. There is darkness within all of us—places of our deepest self that we avoid or don't wish to acknowledge. These are not "bad" things, but many people are ashamed of them—they are most often things such as fears, regrets, bad habits, or guilt. If these "dark" places are not explored from time to time, acknowledged, and dealt with, these issues can cause emotional and even physical suffering. The dark moon is a good time for soul-searching and promoting self-acceptance.

Often the rituals performed during the dark moon involve meditation and contemplation, preparing for the upcoming moon cycle. Sometimes these spells and rituals combine dark and new moon aspects—a change, a new beginning, or leaving behind something to embrace something else.

WAX COLOR: Black or white.

TIMING: Create or burn these candles when the moon is in last waning stage or completely dark.

INGREDIENTS: Add two drops of eucalyptus essential oil (associated with feminine energy, water element, and the moon).

DARK MOON CHANT: *Moonlight hidden from my view,*
Still your presence remains true.
Dark moon help me seek and find—
Show what's in my soul and mind.

If possible, allow these candles to sit outside in the dark overnight (bring them inside before sunrise) or leave them outside for just a few hours. Try to keep the candles out of direct sunlight.

New Moon Candles

The time of the new moon is a time of new beginnings. This is a time of increase, as the moon begins to grow toward fullness, and the new moon sets the stage for the process of the waxing moon phase. This is an ideal time to begin drawing something to you or increasing a particular influence in your life.

WAX COLOR: White.

TIMING: Make these candles when you begin to see the slimmest crescent moon in the sky. You can consult an almanac for the new moon time in your area and make them after the exact moment of new moon if you wish. If you plan to use them in a spell for a fresh start, make them the actual day of the new moon or the next day. (See Chapter 4 for more details on the difference between new moon and dark moon.)

INGREDIENTS: Two drops of eucalyptus essential oil.

NEW MOON CHANT: *Moonlight new, time to start,*
See the need that's in my heart.
Help me reach the goal I seek,
Hear the wish I long to speak.

Allow the candles to sit outside beneath the crescent moon if possible, or near a window. When you light the candle, state your wish, desire, need, or prayer out loud.

A Cycle of Healing with Moon Energy

Use three candles, one each for the dark moon, new moon, and full moon. Begin by lighting the dark moon candle a day or two before the actual new moon. If possible, allow this candle to burn out completely in one night or two, before the new moon. Meditate on banishing negativity and contemplate your deepest self. Confront issues you've been hiding from yourself. On the new moon, acknowledge a fresh start, a time of self-acceptance and love. Burn your new moon candle for a short time each night as the moon waxes to full, continuing to meditate on the changes you're making in your life. Be sure to carry out these changes in the real world. Don't just think about them—take action. At the full moon, light a candle to celebrate. Bask in the light of the full moon and rejoice with self-healing energy. Repeat this ritual as necessary each lunar cycle.

Waxing and Waning Moon Phases

Create these candles on the first and last quarter moon, in waxing or waning stage.

Waxing—a pinch of sandalwood powder—Maiden—any kind of positive magic or ritual.

Waning—two drops of lemon essential oil—Crone—banishing and binding magic.

Use white wax for both, stirring waxing moon candles clockwise and waning moon candles counterclockwise. Burn at the appropriate time for your specific ritual or spell. The waxing phase is a time to draw things toward you or do magic for growth and increasing certain qualities. The waning phase is the best time to work magic of a decreasing nature or for banishing something. It is a time of release and letting go of unwanted or unnecessary influences, obstacles, or harmful energy. You can carve appropriate moon symbols on the bottom of the finished candles to designate which phase each is for—a crescent shaped like the letter *C* is a waning moon; a crescent shaped like the letter *D* is a waxing moon.

Blue Moon Candle

You've heard the phrase that something only happens "once in a blue moon," which implies that this is some type of rare celestial event. Actually, a blue moon usually occurs every two or three years, and you can look for it by checking any calendar that accurately gives moon phases and times. Because our calendar has twelve months and there are thirteen lunar months in a year, sometimes two full moons occur in a month—of course, for this to happen, the first full moon must appear on the first or second day of a long month; the second one will occur at the end.

This recipe is intended to create one large candle on the day or night of a blue moon. You will then save this candle to only burn on future blue moon nights. Or, since the blue moon is basically just a full moon (although magical practitioners ascribe extra power to it), make a batch of full moon candles and consider them to be extra special. You can add a touch of blue wax to the white if you'd like.

Follow the directions for full moon candles on pages 116–117, but use this chant in addition to or in place of the chant for full moon candles:

BLUE MOON CHANT: *Blue Moon magic in the air,*
Blue Moon with your face so rare—
Send your light into this spell,
Energy to serve me well.
Blue Moon on this special night,
Touch these candles with your light.
Guide me with your glowing rays,
Power for all future days.

On the day I'm writing this, it's the blue moon of December 31, 2009. The last time I made candles, I ended up with a chunk of dark blue wax left over. I chipped off some of that, added it to this white wax, and was able to create a candle in a nice shade of pale blue in honor of the blue moon. In addition, I made seven white full moon candles to be used for full moon celebrations throughout the next year; I will keep the light blue candle to be specifically used for a future blue moon. In addition, you can make a large blue moon candle and burn it just for a few hours on blue moon nights. The full moon candles I created today will have bit of extra energy.

Black Moon Candle

In Chapter 4, I mentioned a lesser-known phase called the black moon. Similar to the concept of a blue moon, the black moon is the second *new* moon in a month. If this timing occurs, feel free to use your creativity to de-sign either a special new or dark moon candle to be used for a special ritual or spell. This would be a very good time for deeply introspective magic and big life changes. Simply follow the same directions for the new or dark moon candles on pages 117–120, recognizing that, just as the blue moon is a special full moon, this phase has special significance as well.

Here is a general chant you can use for a black moon candle, or any moon ritual:

MOON CHANT: *Cycles of life,*
waxing, waning.
Success and strife,
waxing, waning.
Tides of power,
waxing, waning.
Seed to flower,
waxing, waning.
Circle bright,
waxing, waning.
Dark to light,
waxing, waning.

Sun Candles

Solar candles can be created during any moon phase, but you may consider the specific use of the candle in order to make a decision. For example, if you know you're going to do magic to increase something in your life, select a waxing moon day or, for decreasing something, select a waning moon day. As with other candles you create, what's probably more important here is the timing of when you burn the candle. In addition, you may wish to consider which sign of the zodiac the sun is in.

Make sun candles on a sunny day, especially on a Sunday. Make sure you have the ability to allow these candles to harden in sunlight—indoors near a window or outside works well.

Sun Candle

WAX COLOR: Yellow is the best color choice, but white, orange, or red are also appropriate colors.

INGREDIENTS: Add a pinch of ground frankincense resin.

Stir in a clockwise motion while visualizing powerful rays of sunlight infusing the wax with energy.

SUN CHANT: *Sunlight strong, day-star bright,*
These candles symbolize your light.
Glow like fire, day or night,
Lend your power to these rites.

Let the candles harden in sunlight, either outside or near a sunny window. These candles can be used to represent a god (or masculine energy) on your altar, or they can be used in any spell that calls for sun energy, especially spells for healing and success, or even solstice celebrations.

Eclipse Candles

A partial or total lunar eclipse occurs when the moon is temporarily obscured from our view by Earth's shadow. A solar eclipse occurs when the moon is situated between the sun and Earth, thus blocking our view of the sun. Ancient peoples were disturbed by these phenomena, until they studied the sky and learned such events could be predicted. Naturally, until the explanation was discovered, many myths and legends were created to explain this rare occurrence. Since these are times of celestial alignment between Earth, moon, and sun, there is a variety of magical energy you can work with. Use candles you have previously created, or take advantage of this time to create candles for future magical use.

Lunar Eclipse Candle

The magical energy surrounding a lunar eclipse is considered to be fickle. It can be used to facilitate change, balance, or to explore all the moon phases at once—similar to the passage of an entire month in a short moment. Create these candles during an eclipse in your area, or elsewhere (consult an almanac for exact dates and times). A lunar eclipse can only occur when the moon is in the full phase, so be aware that you're working with lunar energy at its height. Earth's shadow obscures the moon, so you are working with the influence of both Earth energy and moon energy, which are both feminine.

These candles would be good to use in magic of any kind associated with feminine energy, psychic ability, and bringing about change. Use white or yellow wax; burn them anytime. No ingredients are necessary.

LUNAR ECLIPSE CHANT: *Briefly now your light is masked*
from our earthly view.
This alignment comes to pass,
rare and seen by few.
Power of this special time,
fill this candle I design.

Repeat this chant twice. As you stir in a clockwise motion, visualize the particular energy of this eclipse. If you know you'll be using the candle(s) for a specific purpose, focus on that intent as well. If not, simply see this wax being empowered with this potent lunar energy.

Solar Eclipse Candle

A solar eclipse can only occur in the daytime during a new moon. Of course, these occur at different times and places all over the world. You can wait for one to happen in your area, or you can draw on the influence of a solar eclipse that is occurring elsewhere. You can find this information by consulting a reliable almanac. As with the lunar eclipse representing an entire month in a short time, a solar eclipse symbolizes the passage of an entire year in a short time. Draw on the particular seasonal energy that is present and use it for your specific need. Create these candles during an eclipse to "capture" this energy for future use.

Like lunar eclipse candles, these candles would be useful for magic to bring about change. In addition, these candles combine masculine and feminine energies, so they would be good to use in spells for balance. Since you will be drawing on new moon energy at this time, you can use these candles in spells for new beginnings. Use white wax; burn anytime. No ingredients needed.

SOLAR ECLIPSE CHANT: *Briefly now your light is masked*
from our earthly view.
This alignment comes to pass,
Rare and seen by few.
Power of this special time,
Fill this candle I design.

For this candle, speak the chant only once. As you stir the wax clockwise, visualize your intent. Focus on the balance of solar and lunar energy.

Planetary and Zodiac Candles

The predictions and horoscopes in modern newspapers and magazines are a poor example of the real, and ancient, study of astrology. This study of the sky is the basis of our current science of astronomy. The study of astrology spread over the world and evolved in different ways—the system in the East is different from ours in the West—but the basic belief that the position of the stars and planets can affect us has not faded.

The Egyptians and the Greeks made major contributions to this field; for them, astrology was even linked to the practice of medicine. Pythagoras was a Greek mystic who also studied numbers. He and his followers believed that the heavens could influence occurrences on Earth. We mainly remember him for his contributions to mathematics, as science and reason eventually supplanted mystical beliefs and practices. Nevertheless, astrology and numerology paved the way for many discoveries in science.

A popular phrase in occult and magical practice is "As above, so below," which originated in Hermetic philosophy and expresses the belief that what is above us, in the sky, corresponds to what is below, here on Earth—that there is a connection with what happens in our world and what is going on in the heavens. Through understanding of one, you can understand the other.

Even psychologist Carl Jung consulted horoscopes with his patients and acknowledged that the signs of the zodiac could be seen as human archetypes, playing a significant role in human understanding and self-awareness. He was interested in synchronicity—the meaningful pattern of events—and this term is often found in magical practice. If all things are connected and patterns can be found, our understanding of existence can be explored on a deeper level.

While much has changed over the ages as humans have studied the sky, we can still gain some personal insight by looking into this realm. Remember, magical correspondences are most commonly based on ancient myths and folklore, which have roots in culture and human nature, so we can explore and use this path along the way to deeper understanding of ourselves and the world. Whether you regard astrology as fact or fancy, it has been with us for centuries and will no doubt continue to be examined and explored. Humans are seekers, after all.

Depending on your need, you may want a candle for a specific planetary influence or astrological sign. Keep in mind that the astrological significance of a planet is not the same thing as the "personality" of the deity with the same name. The planets were named in honor of gods and goddesses, such as Venus, Mars, and Saturn, but this doesn't necessarily give the planetary influence the same correspondences as the deity it was named for. Sometimes the influence corresponds, but not always.

Planetary Candles

WAX COLOR: Use a base of white wax and add ingredients based on the lists given, or choose a color based on an astrological sign.

TIMING: When creating and burning the candle, be sure the timing is appropriate for the planet (see Chapter 4).

INGREDIENTS—PLANETS: Here are some of the associated aromas to be used with particular planets and astrological signs. Note that many are shared by more than one and that characteristics of aromas are not necessarily the same as the characteristics of the actual plant. This list pertains to fragrances only—either the essential oil, resin, or aroma of the plant.

To use these, anoint your candle with the oil, or place a few drops in the pool of melted wax near the wick and inhale the scent, visualizing your goal.

☀ **SUN—SUNDAY**

Cedar, cinnamon, copal, frankincense, juniper, orange, rosemary
Uses: protection, healing, success, energy

☾ **MOON—MONDAY**

Eucalyptus, camphor, jasmine, lemon, lily, sandalwood
Uses: psychic ability, dreams, love, fertility, peace, meditation, spirituality, emotions

☿ **MERCURY—WEDNESDAY**

Benzoin, mint, dill, lavender, parsley
Uses: conscious mind, intellect, communication, study, travel, breaking bad habits

♀ **VENUS—FRIDAY**

Apple, chamomile, freesia, gardenia, geranium, hyacinth, iris, lilac, mugwort (plant), rose, thyme, vanilla, yarrow, ylang-ylang
Uses: love, fidelity, beauty, youth, happiness, friendship

♂ **MARS—TUESDAY**

Basil (plant), coriander, cumin, garlic, ginger, pine
Uses: courage, sexual energy, politics, protection, magical energy, healing, aggression, strength

♃ **JUPITER—THURSDAY**

Clove, honeysuckle, mace, nutmeg, sage (plant), star anise
Uses: prosperity, expansion, foundations

♄ SATURN—SATURDAY

Cypress, myrrh, patchouli

Uses: longevity, purification, grounding, wisdom

Uranus, Neptune, and Pluto were not known to the ancient peoples. They were discovered in the eighteenth, nineteenth, and twentieth centuries, respectively. Recently, Pluto was reclassified as a "dwarf" planet by astronomers. You may wish to research the presence of these planets in your natal chart, since astrologers indicate their influence affects specific generations. Folklore and correspondences related to these planets is not abundant, but here are some characteristics to consider when working with these planets:

URANUS: disruptive or sudden change; Aquarius

NEPTUNE: cloudiness, confusion, uncertainty; Pisces

PLUTO: elimination; Scorpio

Zodiac Candles

For magical birthday gifts, to evoke characteristics of a particular sign, or when the moon is in a specific sign, combine as many correspondences as you wish. See each sign for wax color. Create these candles when the sun or moon is in the proper sign; consult a yearly almanac for detailed astronomical information.

♈ ARIES

The Ram, The Warrior; Mars; fire

March 21–April 19

Wax Color: red, pink

Ingredients: clove, coriander, cumin, frankincense, ginger, pine

Uses: adventurous spirit, self-awareness

♉ TAURUS

The Bull, sensuality; Venus; earth

April 20–May 21

Wax Color: green, yellow, pink, light blue

Ingredients: apple, honeysuckle, lilac, patchouli, rose, thyme (plant)

Uses: determination, devotion

♊ GEMINI

The Twins, communication; Mercury; air

May 22–June 21

Wax Color: yellow, violet, red

Ingredients: benzoin, mint, dill, lavender, lemongrass

Uses: thoughtful, social

♋ CANCER

The Crab, home; the moon; water

June 22–July 22

Wax Color: silver, gray, green, pastel colors

Ingredients: chamomile, jasmine, lemon, lily, myrrh, rose, sandalwood, yarrow

Uses: moon magic, hearth and home energy, emotion

♌ LEO

The Lion, self/ego; the sun; fire

July 23–August 23

Wax Color: gold, orange, red, green

Ingredients: bay, basil (plant), cinnamon, frankincense, ginger, juniper, orange, rosemary

Uses: bravery, charisma

♍ VIRGO

The Virgin, practical; Mercury; earth

August 24–September 23

Wax Color: blue, gray, green, violet, gold, yellow

Ingredients: cypress, dill, lemon balm, honeysuckle, patchouli

Uses: logic, accountability

♎ LIBRA

The Scales, The Peacemaker; Venus; air

September 24–October 23

Wax Color: rose, blue, yellow, light green, light blue

Ingredients: chamomile, dill, eucalyptus, geranium, peppermint, pine, vanilla

Uses: balance, peace, beauty

♏ SCORPIO

The Scorpion, desire; Mars and Pluto; water
October 24–November 22
Wax Color: red, black, maroon, brown
Ingredients: hyacinth, pine, thyme (plant)
Uses: creativity, competitive spirit

♐ SAGITTARIUS

The Archer, knowledge; Jupiter; fire
November 23–December 21
Wax Color: purple, dark blue, gold, red
Ingredients: clove, lemon balm, mace, nutmeg, rosemary
Uses: outgoing, open-minded

♑ CAPRICORN

The Goat, career; Saturn; earth
December 22–January 20
Wax Color: brown, dark blue, dark green, red
Ingredients: cypress, honeysuckle, lilac, myrrh, patchouli, tulip
Uses: moderation, gentleness, fidelity

♒ AQUARIUS

The Water-Bearer, groups; Saturn and Uranus; air
January 21–February 19
Wax Color: bright blue, indigo, lavender, green

Ingredients: lavender, parsley, patchouli, pine, star anise

Uses: optimism, originality, enthusiasm

♓ PISCES

The Fish, spiritual; Jupiter and Neptune; water

February 20–March 20

Wax Color: green, turquoise, pale violet, white, mauve

Ingredients: apple, camphor, gardenia, hyacinth, jasmine, lily, mugwort
(plant), myrrh, sandalwood, vanilla

Uses: empathy, instinct, adaptability

Moon in the Signs

Consider the influence of the moon as it passes through the signs of the zodiac.

ARIES: A good time for beginning projects, but better for short-term endeavors. A good time for overcoming obstacles quickly.

TAURUS: A time of resourcefulness. Projects begun at this time have the tendency to last and increase in solidarity. Stability. Money issues.

GEMINI: A time of transformation, but sometimes things begun at this time are easily altered by outside influences. A good time for communication. Business. Entertainment.

CANCER: A good sign for moon magic and stimulating emotions. Domestic matters, growth, and nurturing qualities.

LEO: A good time for developing personal skills and learning. Arts and entertainment. Healing. Courage.

VIRGO: A good time for attention to detail and order. Practicality and success. Verbal and written expression.

LIBRA: A good time for balance, cooperation, beautification, and social events. Favors partnership and decision making. Harmony. Innovation.

SCORPIO: A good time for transformation, self-exploration, and making decisions. Passion, psychic awareness, and emotional openness.

SAGITTARIUS: A time to encourage imagination and confidence. Favors expansion and optimism. Travel. Social interaction.

CAPRICORN: A good time to develop structure or focus on tradition, obligations, and stability. Business, money, grounding, success.

AQUARIUS: A good time for personal change, freedom, and individuality. Intellect.

PISCES: Focus on dreaming, intuition, creativity, and psychic ability. Spirituality. Contemplation.

8 | Spell Candles

Magic is believing in yourself, if you can do that, you can make anything happen.

—JOHANN WOLFGANG VON GOETHE

A spell can be written for just about any purpose you can imagine, but I've found that most of them can be divided into a few major categories. When you're lighting your candle, that's the time to charge it again and focus on your specific situation at that moment. You may want to keep a general need in mind when making a large batch of candles, especially if you know you'll have various uses for them in the future. At other times, all the candles created in a batch will be used for a single purpose, so I'll leave the choice up to you.

When using recycled wax, remember to use the chant and visualization in Chapter 2 to clear the wax of previous energy before adding ingredients and charging the wax for a spell candle.

I have also included information about the specific type of energy and element each spell involves. This is to give you as much information as possible about the nature of each particular style of magic. You may notice that many spells combine aspects of more than one element. Spells can and should be tailored for specific needs, and sometimes that means drawing on a variety of correspondences. Keep this in mind when you create your own candle spells (see Chapter 10). Always consider the main type of element and energy that you will draw on, as this will help the focus of your spell. Also be aware that the focus may change, depending on your situation. A spell for success might be to get an interview for a job, or it may involve trying to secure a promotion at an existing job. You may want a quick change or a long-lasting solution. Always consider your specific needs in order to get the best results.

You might be thinking that all candle magic is associated with the fire element. That's true—in a way, fire applies to all magic since magic transforms and makes change. That's the nature of the element of fire. But the subtle qualities of each spell have associations with other aspects including color, day, time, herbs, and oils. Don't let the correspondences confuse you—they are used for a reason and specific purpose.

In addition, don't be confused by the moon sign if it doesn't appear to go with the elemental style of the spell—these will not necessarily match. For example, Libra is an air sign, yet the moon in Libra is associated with the qualities of earth and water (love, abundance, and fertility) because Libra is ruled by Venus, goddess of love and beauty. The element associated with an astrological sign represents an influence on a person born in that sign, not necessarily the type of magic done during that sign. This might sound complicated, but remember that as long as you keep your intent in mind, you'll do just fine.

Always remember to be patient—spells take time to manifest. It may take longer than you expect to see results and sometimes the outcome is subtle. Remain open to possibilities when working with magic and you will continue to be rewarded in unexpected ways.

Candles for Love and Romance

These candle spells can be used to draw love into your life or to increase the passion or deepen the bonds of affection in an existing, mutual relationship.

Remember: never try to manipulate another person with a love spell. You wouldn't want someone trying to control your emotions. Plus, you may just get what you wish for, with surprising and unintended results!

To Draw Love

WAX COLOR: pink

MOON PHASE TO MAKE/BURN: waxing to full

MOON SIGN TO MAKE/BURN: Libra

BEST DAY TO MAKE/BURN: Friday

ELEMENT AND ENERGY: earth and water; receptive

INGREDIENTS: one dried pink or red rose petal, crumbled into molten wax

CHANT: *Bring to me*
            Love meant to be.

Repeat these words six times while stirring clockwise.

Visualize being happy and in love (but don't picture a specific person). Imagine the wonderful, warm feeling of being in love, of finding just the right person to share experiences with, of having someone bring joy into your life. As you pour each candle, repeat the phrase again. Also repeat it when you light each candle. Burn a group of six of these candles on a Friday night during the waxing moon, and allow them to burn completely. You may want to make half-size votives for this, but it's up to you. You can carve two joined hearts into the wax.

To Increase Affection

WAX COLOR: pink

MOON PHASE TO MAKE/BURN: waxing to full

MOON SIGN TO MAKE/BURN: Libra or Cancer

BEST DAY TO MAKE/BURN: Friday or Monday

ELEMENT AND ENERGY: earth and water; receptive

INGREDIENTS: dried pink or red rose petals, whole

In the bottom of the candle mold, place one dried pink or red rose petal. Coat the petal with wax first. After you pour the wax, the rose petal may float to the top. That's OK—when the wax begins to thicken and it's time to add the wick, use a wick with a metal tab on the bottom to push the petal down, sticking it to the bottom of the mold with the wick tab.

CHANT: *If it be true,*
              Our love renew.

Repeat these words ten times while stirring clockwise.

You may make several of these candles, but only burn one for the spell—this represents unity, and in this spell you're striving to renew an existing relationship. Beware: in a struggling relationship, it's possible that renewing is not best for everyone involved. You're not seeking to manipulate another person, but rather to deepen a mutual bond, if both people are willing. As you pour, visualize becoming closer to your partner, reviving the spark of romance. Begin burning this candle on a Friday night during a waxing moon and if it doesn't burn out that night, keep burning it each day until it's spent. Make a full-size paper cup candle for this spell, or use a juice can. Carve the symbol of joined wedding rings into the wax, or one heart. Repeat the phrase as you light the candle. If you made several candles, save the others to burn on future Friday nights during the waxing moon. Repeat this process until you see results. Of course, don't forget to talk to your partner and work on the relationship in a practical way as well. If your partner is willing, the two of you can light the candle together and say the phrase together, as a promise to work through difficulties and strengthen your relationship.

To Spark Passion

WAX COLOR: red

MOON PHASE TO MAKE/BURN: waxing to full

MOON SIGN TO MAKE/BURN: Scorpio

BEST DAY TO MAKE/BURN: Tuesday or Friday

ELEMENT AND ENERGY: fire; projective

INGREDIENTS: a pinch of dried dill and/or dried parsley (herbs to inspire lust) and essential oils, as desired, during the burning process

CHANT: *Passion's spark, excite, ignite;*
           revive our touch—make it right.

Chant this nine times while stirring clockwise.

This spell is intended to cause change to a current situation. Imagine the heat of passion like electricity between you and your partner. Again, if he or she is willing, both of you can participate in lighting the candle and repeating the phrase. Or use these candles for a romantic candlelight dinner and see what happens!

Experiment with the scent you and your partner find most arousing: ginger, jasmine, patchouli, rose, sandalwood, vanilla, or ylang-ylang. Add a few drops to the wax before pouring, anoint the finished candle, and also add a few drops to the wax pool while the candle burns.

The other love candles draw on the earth element for its nurturing qualities; this one is ruled by the element of fire. It's a different kind of energy, so use this spell to fan the flames of desire with someone you trust.

Binding and Banishing

You can defend yourself by neutralizing harmful energy. Rather than trying to cause harm to someone, you are aiming to protect yourself and leaving the rest to the universe. To bind someone from doing harm is one way to protect yourself if someone is causing you pain or discomfort. This action is intended to deter someone's harmful words or intent. Always seek help from authorities if you are in serious danger or facing a personal threat.

To banish someone from your life is a stronger step than binding. Banishing should be used if the situation is more severe than mere annoyance. If you feel threatened by the words or actions of another person, banishing is a way to block their influence in your life by separating them from you rather than just binding their actions. Sometimes binding and banishing are used together.

Several years ago, some neighborhood kids vandalized my house. The police took action, but I took steps of my own. In addition to increasing mundane protection around my home, I performed a spell of binding and banishing. I wanted to keep them from harming anyone else's property or mine, but I also wanted them out of my life. They had been causing other problems in the neighborhood. If the problems these kids had been causing were simply minor annoyances, a binding spell may have been enough to block their actions. But since they did actual harm to my home, I wanted them out of my life and the neighborhood. It worked. A month later, the family moved away.

Binding

WAX COLOR: black or white

MOON PHASE TO MAKE/BURN: waning

MOON SIGN TO MAKE/BURN: Taurus or Capricorn

BEST DAY TO MAKE/BURN: Saturday

ELEMENT AND ENERGY: earth; receptive

INGREDIENTS: a pinch of powdered frankincense and a pinch of dragon's blood resin (optional); place one pine needle in each candle mold—if the pine needle floats to the top when you add the wax, use a wick with a tab at the bottom to press it down and secure it to the bottom of the mold

Stir the molten wax in a counterclockwise direction eight times while visualizing your intent.

Obtain something that represents the person you wish to bind—such as a photo, signature, personal object, strand of hair, etc.—or just write that person's name or address on a piece of paper. Light the candle and, as the wax begins to pool around the wick, tilt the candle so the liquid wax drips on the photo or other item. Visualize this person being unable to do harm to you in any way. Allow the wax to cool on the item, then complete the spell by wrapping the wax-encrusted item with a black ribbon or thread. Continue your visualization as you wrap.

If you suspect someone of having harmful intent toward you but you're unsure, try this conditional binding spell. Speak this chant four times:

If her/his/their intent be ill,
Let this be my will—
If she/he/they mean(s) to cause me harm,
Activate this charm.
Help me clear the air,
Help me be aware.

If you need this spell for an area where you can't burn a candle, such as at work or school, create the candle and use it to empower an object that you can keep in the environment where you suspect the threat. For example, if you are suspicious of someone at work gossiping about you and trying to sabotage your position, find a picture or hex symbol that you can hang on the wall and burn a protection or binding candle on top of it to charge it. Then hang or place the item in your work space. If it's not possible to put the item in a visible place, keep the item with you, such as in a purse or wallet, or keep it in a desk drawer or locker.

Banishment

WAX COLOR: white, red, or black

MOON PHASE TO MAKE/BURN: waning

MOON SIGN TO MAKE/BURN: Aries or Leo

BEST DAY TO MAKE/BURN: Tuesday or Sunday

ELEMENT AND ENERGY: fire; projective

INGREDIENTS: a pinch of ground cloves, a pinch of powdered frankincense, and a pinch of dried rosemary

Stir in a counterclockwise motion eight times. Visualize the unwanted presence departing from your life in a peaceful manner that is beneficial to everyone. Before lighting the candle, anoint it with pine essential oil.

After the candle cools, carve the name of the person you wish to banish into the wax, then draw an X or slash through the name. When you visualize, make sure you imagine that person leaving your environment—unless you desire to be moved from that person. For example, you could wish to banish a co-worker and end up being transferred elsewhere yourself! The spell worked, that person is out of your life, but you ended up being moved. If you don't desire that outcome, be sure to visualize yourself remaining where you are and the other person moving on. Do this for that person's highest good, without causing harm.

To Increase Prosperity and Abundance

Prosperity, wealth, and abundance should not be considered a greedy goal. We all need a certain amount of prosperity in our lives—we must be able to eat, get around, and have shelter. Don't feel bad if you would like a little more than the bare necessities, as everyone deserves to have a comfortable life. The only downfall is when a person puts material success over well-being and personal relationships.

These candles are intended to help you focus on good spending habits, bringing prosperity to your life, and paying off debts. Keep those goals in mind and understand that the odds are against you winning the lottery, but more in favor of making sure you are provided with everything you need—and perhaps a little extra from time to time.

You can make several of these and burn one each month during the waxing moon.

WAX COLOR: green

MOON PHASE TO MAKE/BURN: waxing to full

MOON SIGN TO MAKE/BURN: Taurus (or Cancer for domestic matters)

BEST DAY TO MAKE/BURN: Thursday or Friday

ELEMENT AND ENERGY: earth; receptive

INGREDIENTS: a pinch of ground cinnamon or cloves, a pinch of dried basil or dried mint leaves, and two drops of peppermint oil

Stir the wax in a clockwise direction and chant twice:

Money, money, come to me,
as I will so mote it be.
Grant my wish, fulfill my need,
I ask this out of love, not greed.

Visualize your need—bills being paid, abundance, etc. Remember: visualizing winning the lottery won't help you. Keep your goals modest and realistic. When you pour the candles, place a coin in the bottom of mold, if you wish. Alternately, you can add a coin to the bottom of the container when you burn the candle, if you don't want to add the coin now. Either option is fine. You may also carve a dollar sign into the finished candle and anoint it with a drop of pine oil before burning.

Protection

These candles can be used in protection spells for yourself, your home, or anything else you need to guard.

WAX COLOR: red or white

MOON PHASE TO MAKE/BURN: waxing to full

MOON SIGN TO MAKE/BURN: Aries, Taurus, or Leo

BEST DAY TO MAKE/BURN: Tuesday or Sunday

ELEMENT AND ENERGY: fire and earth; projective

INGREDIENTS: rose thorns and/or sea salt, a pinch of dried dill, and five drops essential oil of geranium, mint, or pine

Place one rose thorn in the bottom of the mold. Again, as with the rose petal, the thorn may float to the top. When the wax begins to thicken, press it down with a wick that has a metal tab. Another option is to grind dried thorns using a mortar and pestle and sprinkle them into the molten wax. You can also sprinkle a thin layer of sea salt into the bottom of the mold.

CHANT: *Protect and keep, safely guard,*
          As I will, create this ward.

Stir the wax in a clockwise direction while visualizing a shield around your home, property, or other area you wish to guard. You can also visualize yourself dressed in protective armor. Continue the visualization when you burn the candle.

You may want to use a juice can to make larger candles for this spell. Using the "paint" technique in Chapter 10, you can decorate these candles with a pentacle symbol or try one of the other decorative options listed below.

Decorative options: brush the outside of the finished candle with a thin layer of wax and roll the candle in coarse salt. Brush on a wax pentacle and quickly, before the wax hardens, press salt grains into the design. Remember: if you choose to decorate the outside of your candle, use a small wick so a well burns down through the center of the candle and does not melt the outside. If you use a larger mold, such as a juice can, a medium wick should work well.

Purification

These candles are perfect to burn for cleansing harmful or unwanted energy from your environment or yourself. Use during meditation or burn one in each room of your home. You can use these in conjunction with the protection candles, especially when moving into a new home. These are also good candles to burn as you prepare sacred space for a ritual.

WAX COLOR: white

MOON PHASE TO MAKE/BURN: anytime

MOON SIGN TO MAKE/BURN: any

BEST DAY TO MAKE/BURN: anytime

ELEMENT AND ENERGY: water or fire; receptive (cleansing self) or projective (clearing a space)

INGREDIENTS: a pinch of dried rosemary or sage, three drops cedarwood essential oil

If you dislike the smoke associated with smudging a room, you can burn one of these candles and add a few drops of essential oil (rosemary or cedar) to the molten wax pool. This will release the fragrance. Burn these in the room as you bathe or shower to enhance a purification bath.

Stir the wax counterclockwise and add the ingredients. Visualize cleansing and clearing of a particular space or your self.

CHANT: *Renew and clean,*
         Cleanse and clear,
         Let nothing harmful
         Linger here.

If you wish, ring a bell over the molten wax just before pouring, as you visualize dispelling the unwanted energy.

To Break a Bad Habit

WAX COLOR: black or white

MOON PHASE TO MAKE/BURN: waning/dark to new

MOON SIGN TO MAKE/BURN: Scorpio or Aquarius (freedom)

BEST DAY TO MAKE/BURN: Saturday or Sunday

ELEMENT AND ENERGY: fire and water or earth; mainly receptive

INGREDIENTS: add three of drops of lavender essential oil to the molten wax

Visualize the bad habit you're trying to break as you stir the wax counterclockwise. See yourself being free of whatever burden is hanging over you. If it helps, speak out loud the change you're trying to make in your life. Then add the oil and stir the wax counterclockwise.

Say the full chant once and repeat the last line ten more times:

What holds me back or causes fear
Harms me, keeps me
Prisoner here.
Unbind, release, and set me free,
Break the tie(s) that hinder(s) me.

These candles are best used for personal transformation. After the candle has cooled, use it in a spell by writing the bad habit you're trying to change on a piece of paper. Put the paper in a heatproof container and place the candle on top of it. Allow the wax to melt over the paper and, when the candle is spent, discard the wax and paper. It's best to throw these items away in a place other than your home. Find a public waste can or dumpster.

Healing

Much like the nature of breaking a bad habit, healing can take the form of using the nurturing qualities of earth and water or the transformative power of fire. Often these elements are combined for spells that involve change to the self, since the energy required is ultimately receptive, but fire has a projective quality. Sometimes a practitioner may prefer to focus on fire for building strength, earth for a healthy body, or water for its nurturing qualities. This particular spell is intended for general vitality and combines the elements of fire and water.

WAX COLOR: white, blue, green, or yellow/orange

MOON PHASE TO MAKE/BURN: waxing

MOON SIGN TO MAKE/BURN: an earth or water sign

BEST DAY TO MAKE/BURN: Sunday or Monday

ELEMENT AND ENERGY: all elements apply, especially earth and water; receptive

INGREDIENTS: to the molten wax add a pinch of dried chamomile flowers and a pinch of any combination of the following dried/ground herbs: cinnamon, rosemary, thyme, sage, mint, pine, frankincense, or lavender; you can also use a sun candle for this spell

Visualize healing energy, like beams of light, infusing the wax as you stir in a clockwise motion. Or, visualize the nurturing arms of Mother Earth embracing you.

Say the entire chant once and repeat the last two lines seven more times:

To be well
Is to be whole,
Heal body, mind, and soul.
This is my shield.
I shall be healed.

Save these candles to burn anytime you need a boost of energy or when you need help healing. You can also burn these candles as part of a healing meditation or during a yoga sequence, while visualizing beams of light filling you and burning away any illness or discomfort. Always seek medical attention for illness when appropriate.

Success

Success means something different to everyone. If you plan to make a batch of these candles with a general focus, you can simply think of achieving goals and having self-confidence. However, if you have a specific goal in mind—finding employment, going on an interview, enhancing your current job satisfaction, or preparing for an exam of some kind—you can focus on that and just make one or two candles. You can also use sun candles for a success spell; just visualize your intent when you light the candle. Naturally, you must be doing everything you can in a practical way to ensure your success as well. This may involve training, updating your resumé, studying with a tutor, and so on.

COLOR: yellow, orange, or white

MOON PHASE TO MAKE/BURN: waxing to full

MOON SIGN TO MAKE/BURN: Aquarius for personal change; Gemini for quick transformation or business; Capricorn or Taurus for stability; Leo for learning and courage; Sagittarius for travel and confidence

BEST DAY TO MAKE/BURN: Wednesday (business, memory and mental skills, networking) or Sunday (leadership, power)

ELEMENT AND ENERGY: air or earth; projective or receptive (earth governs stability and employment and is receptive; air rules mental skills and is projective)

INGREDIENTS: to the molten wax add a pinch of dried oak leaves, five drops of lavender, and two drops of orange essential oil (orange is generally uplifting and positive; lavender is ruled by Mercury, whose influence covers communication and mental skills; oak is for good fortune)

Visualize your intent as you stir the molten wax in a clockwise motion. Chant three times:

As I work
I plant the seed.
In my goals
I will succeed.
As I plan
I learn and grow
The more I strive
Results will show.

Create an altar dedicated to your goal by arranging an even number of candles on the altar and including something that represents your goal— a newspaper ad, photo, or other document or item. Add a piece of citrine quartz. Beginning on a Wednesday, burn the candles for a few hours on consecutive nights during a waxing moon phase until they are spent or until you know the outcome of your endeavor.

Fertility

Fertility doesn't necessarily mean giving birth. Of course, this spell can be used if you are trying to get pregnant, but a fertility spell can also be used for a garden or to promote growth in other ways, such as creative projects, fostering a nurturing environment, or hoping for a successful adoption of a child or even of a pet. Focus on your specific need as you create these candles, or just envision a nurturing quality as you create a batch to be charged later.

WAX COLOR: white or green

MOON PHASE TO MAKE/BURN: new, waxing, or full

MOON SIGN TO MAKE/BURN: Libra or Cancer

BEST DAY TO MAKE/BURN: Friday

ELEMENT AND ENERGY: earth and water; receptive

INGREDIENTS: dried geranium flowers or pine cone

Find a natural pine cone (one that is free of any perfumes or dyes) and crush it. Add a bit of the crushed cones to the molten wax. Alternately, you can use a pinch of dried geranium flowers. Stir the wax clockwise and visualize your need.

Chant six times:

Grow and flourish,
Bear great fruit.
This goal of mine
Will now take root.

You can burn these candles while you're working on a project or as a celebration of a birth or adoption. Write your goal on a piece of paper or use a picture and set the candleholder on top of it.

Mental Clarity and Intellect/Communication

We all experience moments when we wish we could be more eloquent, know just what to say and when to speak, and be able to recall information quickly. Such skills are important in many situations, and these candles are designed to help you focus, communicate effectively, and improve your memory.

You may be wondering why a spell for intellect is considered projective energy if it is intended to affect the self. This is because the nature of air spells involves sending thoughts and ideas out into the universe. The end result is to share your knowledge and use it, which is ultimately a projective act. Even if you desire creative energy to make something, you will undoubtedly end up sharing your creation in some way. It begins within you, but ends up as an outward projection of your inspiration, talent, and effort.

WAX COLOR: white or yellow

MOON PHASE TO MAKE/BURN: waxing to full

MOON SIGN TO MAKE/BURN: Aquarius, Virgo, or Sagittarius

BEST DAY TO MAKE/BURN: Wednesday

ELEMENT AND ENERGY: air; projective

INGREDIENTS: lavender essential oil or peppermint

Add five drops of essential oil of lavender or peppermint and stir the wax clockwise as you visualize your specific need.

Chant five times:

Let my thoughts and words be clear,
May I listen not just hear;
May I speak profound and true,
Let my mind be sharp and new.

Burn these candles while working on a creative project or while preparing for a situation where you need to focus. You may also use these candles during meditation.

To Build Courage and Strength

Courage and strength are required in different ways throughout our lives. We can require these skills emotionally or physically. To increase both, use these candles.

WAX COLOR: red or white

MOON PHASE TO MAKE/BURN: waxing to full

MOON SIGN TO MAKE/BURN: Leo, Capricorn, or Aries

BEST DAY TO MAKE/BURN: Tuesday or Sunday

ELEMENT AND ENERGY: fire; projective

INGREDIENTS: a pinch of ground cloves

Stir the wax in a clockwise motion as you visualize your need.
Chant:

Give me strength, let it endure,
Know my motives that are pure.
Courage be my aide and guide,
Help me grow, not give me pride.

Carry a piece of the spent candle wax with you as a talisman.

Creativity and Inspiration

Everyone needs creativity in life—it's the beautiful self-expression that shows the world who we are. And we can share our creativity in so many ways. For these candles, call on your muse, if you have one, or request the aid of the Nine Muses of classical Greek mythology.

WAX COLOR: white, gold, silver, yellow, violet

MOON PHASE TO MAKE/BURN: waxing to full

MOON SIGN TO MAKE/BURN: Pisces or Virgo

BEST DAY TO MAKE/BURN: Wednesday, Monday, or Sunday

ELEMENT AND ENERGY: air; projective (actually, all elements are useful for creative work—earth for working with your hands, air for verbal expression, water for emotional expression, and fire for the spark of creative energy)

INGREDIENTS: three drops of lavender essential oil or a pinch of ground cinnamon

As you stir, visualize your goal or simply imagine yourself expressing your creativity. If you have a specific project in mind, think of that, or just focus on creativity in general. Stir in a clockwise motion.

Chant three times:

Muses, hear me, my desire
is the spark, creative fire.

Fill this candle with your power,
As I burn it, thoughts will flower.

Burn these candles while you perform creative work or meditate.

Dream Magic

You've undoubtedly heard the advice to "sleep on it" or that "things will look different in the morning." Sleep is one of the most interesting mysteries of the human body. It's more than just a time for rest, as the mind is actually quite active during slumber. Many people believe that we can work through problems and find solutions while we sleep, even if we aren't aware of it. If you're troubled by a difficult decision, need advice, or just need some clarity of thought, use this spell to invite your dreaming mind to help you.

WAX COLOR: white

MOON PHASE TO MAKE/BURN: dark or new to waxing

MOON SIGN TO MAKE/BURN: Pisces

BEST DAY TO MAKE/BURN: Monday

ELEMENT AND ENERGY: water; receptive

INGREDIENTS: a pinch of dried marigold or rose petals (or dried mugwort, if you can find it); jasmine essential oil is also a good choice, but quite expensive

As you stir the molten wax clockwise, visualize sleeping, dreaming, and waking with the clues you need to answer your questions or solve your problems. Know that dreams are symbolic, so it may take time and practice to decipher the messages you receive.

Chant twice:

As I sleep and deeply dream,
Mysteries unfold for me.
Things aren't always what they seem—
Show me what I need to see.

These candles are intended to be burned prior to sleeping (never during) and should be burned in the room you sleep in. About an hour or two before you plan to retire for the night, light these candles in the room, repeat the chant, and use visualization again as you light the candles. Before you go to bed, snuff or blow out the candles.

As you drift off to sleep, raise an issue or question in your mind that you are seeking to resolve. Try not to dwell on it or worry about it—that can keep you awake! Rather, offer it up to your dreaming mind as something to consider while you sleep. Keep paper and pen near your bed so you can write down your dreams upon waking. Repeat the process by relighting the candles each night until they are spent. Keep track of your dreams for several nights to see if patterns or themes emerge.

9 | Candles for Mood and Well-Being

Change your thoughts and you change your world.

—NORMAN VINCENT PEALE

The candles in this chapter are mainly for use in personal rituals. While these aren't exactly spell candles, they are designed to facilitate change. This is change to the self, which can be the most powerful form of magic. As with any spell or ritual, the right state of mind is important. In addition, these candles can be used as gifts or as part of a celebration.

Meditation

What makes this candle special is setting the right mood for its use and creation—your intent. Breathe deeply and know that these candles will help you meditate more effectively. You can use them to focus on while meditating, or just burn them in the room. If you choose aromatherapy while burning, use essential oil of frankincense or sandalwood.

WAX COLOR: white

MOON PHASE TO MAKE/BURN: new or waxing

BEST DAYS TO MAKE/BURN: Monday

MOON SIGN TO MAKE/BURN: Pisces or Cancer

ELEMENT AND ENERGY: water; receptive

INGREDIENTS: a tiny pinch of sandalwood powder

Chant seven times as you stir the wax clockwise:

Deeply down, relax my mind,
Clear all thoughts, I now unwind.
Bring to me a reverent state,
aid me as I meditate.

Create a meditation altar. This is typically a small table where you place items used during meditation to help you concentrate. Many people use candles, crystals, and other objects such as flowers or prayer beads to help relax and focus their mind.

Relaxation

WAX COLOR: white or light blue

MOON PHASE TO MAKE/BURN: new moon

MOON SIGN TO MAKE/BURN: any

BEST DAYS TO MAKE/BURN: any

ELEMENT AND ENERGY: water; receptive

INGREDIENTS: see below

Chant this positive affirmation as you stir the wax clockwise:

I am calm,
Nothing's wrong.
I am calm,
I am strong.

As you pour the wax, envision calmness and serenity. Picture whatever it is that most brings you peace. Imagine your worries melting away or burning away by candle flame.

Also repeat the chant as you light the candle. When burning, add a few drops of relaxing aromatherapy oil to the puddle of wax around the wick. Use lavender or orange, or purchase a blend specifically made for relaxation. Most places that sell real essential oils also sell pure oil blends. Or experiment and make your own blend!

Combine relaxation candles with meditation candles. Burn while doing yoga or other relaxing stretches, or while listening to soothing music. Use these candles in the bathroom as part of a relaxing bath combined with bath salts or essential oils in the water.

Rejuvenation

Sometimes we find ourselves feeling lethargic and in need of a lift. These candles are intended to energize your mind and alleviate fatigue. Ginger has often been used for this purpose, and essential oils of rosemary or cedar are also good options. Choose the scent you like best.

WAX COLOR: yellow or white

MOON PHASE TO MAKE/BURN: waxing to full

BEST DAY TO MAKE/BURN: Sunday

MOON SIGN TO MAKE/BURN: Sagittarius, or any

ELEMENT AND ENERGY: fire and air; projective

INGREDIENTS: a pinch of ginger powder or add a few drops of ginger, cedar, or rosemary essential oil to the wax pool while the candle is burning

Chant nine times while stirring in a clockwise motion:

Revive, renew, and energize!

Carve sun symbols, a smiley face, or whatever cheers you into the finished candles. Smile as you do it! Feel the energy. There's a reason happy people are said to have a sunny disposition. Visualize rays of sunlight making the wax glow with radiant energy. Sprinkle a bit of ginger root in the bottom of the molds, if desired. Also try spearmint or lemongrass essential oils; these are associated with the air element and have uplifting aromas that can help stimulate the mind.

Grounding

If you have too much energy and need to release some, ground it. Grounding is a process of sending excess energy into the earth, which helps you relax and focus. Grounding is often needed after raising energy during magical workings, but sometimes we just feel scattered and need to clear our mind. Grounding is a way of doing this.

WAX COLOR: white, brown, green, or dark blue

MOON PHASE TO MAKE/BURN: any

BEST DAY TO MAKE/BURN: Saturday, or any

MOON SIGN TO MAKE/BURN: Taurus or Capricorn

ELEMENT AND ENERGY: earth; receptive

INGREDIENTS: a few drops of a earthy-scented essential oil such as patchouli or vetivert added to the molten wax or as the candle is burning

Stir the wax in a clockwise motion while visualizing whatever calming image works best for you to ground. A good idea is to imagine your feet as roots of a tree, growing down into the ground. Breathe deeply. Grounding connects you with the earth. Put a tiny stone in the bottom of the mold of each candle, if you wish. Burn these candles to help you "come down" when you feel erratic or stressed and need to dispel excess energy.

Harmony

These candles are designed to promote harmony in your home environment. Burn these in any room to create a calming atmosphere.

WAX COLOR: white, pink

MOON PHASE TO MAKE/BURN: waxing to full

BEST DAY TO MAKE/BURN: Monday

MOON SIGN TO MAKE/BURN: Libra or Cancer

ELEMENT AND ENERGY: air and water; projective

INGREDIENTS: six drops of lavender essential oil and six drops of chamomile essential oil added to molten wax and the puddle of wax around wick while candle is burning

Chant three times:

May these candles be a balm,
Bringing peace and sense of calm.

Stir clockwise and visualize a peaceful atmosphere; continue the visualization when you light these candles. Burn these candles in combination with clusters of quartz crystal, which are often used to enhance a sense of community and unity. These can be placed as accent pieces in the home on shelves or tables.

To Promote Restful Sleep

This candle is not to be confused with the spell candle that promotes dreaming. This candle is designed to give you a restful sleep without encouraging anything out of the ordinary. Remember: always extinguish candles before falling asleep. These candles are intended to be burned in your bedroom as a preparation for sleeping, **not** to be burned *while* you sleep. The goal is to create a relaxing environment that promotes a comfortable place for sleep. If you have recurring difficulty falling or staying asleep, consult a physician.

WAX COLOR: white or any shade of blue

MOON PHASE TO MAKE/BURN: new to waxing

MOON SIGN TO MAKE/BURN: Pisces, Cancer

BEST DAY TO MAKE/BURN: any

ELEMENT AND ENERGY: water; receptive

INGREDIENTS: a few drops of chamomile or lavender essential oil

Chant six times:

Restful sleep be mine.

When you create these candles, visualize restful sleep. Stir in a clockwise motion. Imagine yourself well rested and waking refreshed. You can add the essential oils either during the candle-making process, or to the melted wax pool as you burn the candle.

Easing Grief/Bringing Comfort

These candles can be burned near a photo, burned for someone else, or given as a gift. It's best not to make these candles while in very deep stages of grieving unless you're ready to begin the healing process—wait until you're strong enough. If making candles for future use, make them anytime. Grief can be for loss of a loved one or other life-changing event that causes pain, such as job loss, divorce, or any difficult situation that is hard to accept.

WAX COLOR: white

MOON PHASE TO MAKE/BURN: any

BEST DAY TO MAKE/BURN: any

MOON SIGN TO MAKE/BURN: any

ELEMENT AND ENERGY: water; receptive

INGREDIENTS: a pinch of dried sage leaves

As you stir the wax clockwise, send loving, comforting thoughts—or visualize fond memories. Feel a comforting embrace surround you.

Chant once:

Candle, comfort with your light,
Help me through this darkest night.
Ease this time of loss and pain,
I accept and will sustain.

Spirituality

Use these candles to enhance any spiritual experience.

WAX COLOR: white

MOON PHASE TO MAKE/BURN: dark to new

MOON SIGN TO MAKE/BURN: Pisces, Scorpio

BEST DAY TO MAKE/BURN: any

ELEMENT AND ENERGY: water; receptive

INGREDIENTS: a pinch of any or all of the following: frankincense resin, myrrh resin or sandalwood powder; alternatively, seven drops of any one of these essential oils

Stir clockwise and visualize tranquility, a sense of calm, and a connection with spirit. You may chant any prayer, mantra, or words of your choice that help you attune with a sense of spirituality. These words can be combined with meditation and candles to ease your grief.

Blessings and Gifts

These candles are intended to be gifts for special events such as birthdays, weddings, showers, a new home, and so on. Simply project your desired intent for the event as you stir. Tie a bow around the finished candle. These candles look particularly nice when frosted. Remember to avoid wishing for anything specific, just send good wishes, happiness, etc.

WAX COLOR: white or any color of your choice

MOON PHASE TO MAKE/BURN: waxing to full

BEST DAY TO MAKE/BURN: any

MOON SIGN TO MAKE/BURN: any

Chant once:

Bless this candle, may it bring,
All the best of everything.
Good will, good fortune, fondest dreams—
For good of all, so mote it be.

Chakra Candles

Imagine orbs of energy spinning circles of color like a rainbow within you, beginning at the base of your spine and flowing up to the top of your head. Each of these circles is a kind of energy vortex, a kind of consciousness. The classic chakra system consists of seven of these energy centers located at specific nerve areas of the body. This philosophy has its roots in ancient India. The word *chakra* is Sanskrit and means wheel, disc, or circle. It is believed that by balancing this aspect of the subtle body a person can improve their energy flow, or *prana* (life force), and thus work through difficulties.

The study of the chakra system involves much more than what I have mentioned here, but many people who study a mystical path are interested in exploring this field. These candles are designed to accompany your chakra-balancing work. If you are unfamiliar with the chakras, this information will introduce you to some of the basics.

These candles can be created anytime (I do recommend the full moon), but the most important part of using these candles is your focus. Study each of the seven chakras and their associations, then create a candle for the area(s) you need to work on. Use these candles as part of meditation or healing rituals. If desired, carve the corresponding symbol into the candle (use semicircles if the lotus petal shapes are too much for you) or use the suggested stones either in the candle mold or around the candle while burning. Please note

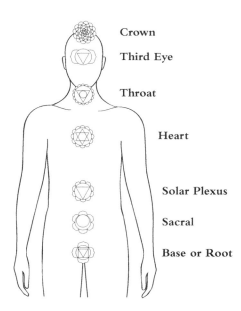

that the elements associated with the chakras don't exactly match the four classical elements mentioned earlier. Those four come from a Western tradition and these elements are from the East. There are some similarities in the systems and also some slight differences. For these candles, follow the correspondences given here.

Each description includes the Sanskrit name of the chakra as well as the English name, its location in the body, element, purpose and issues, color, stones to use, and the symbol used to represent it. Use the color for the candle wax and stir in a clockwise motion. Visualize your intent as you stir and again when you light the candle.

CHAKRA ONE: MULADHARA (ROOT OR BASE)

LOCATION: base of spine

ELEMENT: earth

PURPOSE: grounding, stability, foundation, physical identity, self-preservation

ISSUES: domestic issues, structure, the physical body, health, security, finances

COLOR: red

STONE: agate, bloodstone, tiger's eye, hematite

SYMBOL: red lotus of four petals around a square with a downward-pointing triangle inside

CHAKRA TWO: SVADHISTHANA (SACRAL)

LOCATION: hips, lower back, genitals

ELEMENT: water

PURPOSE: movement

ISSUES: emotions, sexuality, desire

COLOR: orange

STONE: moonstone, citrine, carnelian

SYMBOL: six-petaled lotus, crescent moon inside

CHAKRA THREE: MANIPURA (SOLAR PLEXUS)

LOCATION: solar plexus, abdomen

ELEMENT: fire

PURPOSE: personal power, fulfillment, energy, transformation

ISSUES: individuality, self-esteem, will, vitality

COLOR: yellow

STONE: malachite, aventurine quartz, smoky quartz

SYMBOL: lotus with ten petals, downward-pointing triangle inside

CHAKRA FOUR: ANAHATA (HEART)

LOCATION: heart and chest area

ELEMENT: air

PURPOSE: love, compassion, humanitarianism

ISSUES: balance, self-love, relationships

COLOR: green

STONE: jade, aventurine quartz, rose quartz, emerald

SYMBOL: lotus with twelve petals with a six-pointed star inside (upward and downward-pointing triangles representing the balance of spirit and matter)

CHAKRA FIVE: VISHUDDHA (THROAT)

  LOCATION: throat

  ELEMENT: sound

  PURPOSE: communication and creativity

  ISSUES: self-expression, listening, truth

  COLOR: blue

  STONE: aquamarine, lapis lazuli, turquoise, celestite

  SYMBOL: lotus with sixteen petals, downward-pointing triangle inside
      with a circle at the center

CHAKRA SIX: AJNA (THIRD EYE)

  LOCATION: forehead and brow (third eye)

  ELEMENT: light

  PURPOSE: intuition, insight, sixth sense, psychic powers

  ISSUES: vision, imagination, telepathic energy

  COLOR: indigo

  STONE: amethyst, fluorite, azurite

  SYMBOL: lotus of two petals, downward-pointing triangle inside and in
      the center (the symbol for "ohm")

CHAKRA SEVEN: SAHASRARA (CROWN)

  LOCATION: crown/top of head

  ELEMENT: thought, consciousness

  PURPOSE: awareness, understanding, connection with the Divine

  ISSUES: spirituality, understanding, intelligence, mystical awakening

COLOR: violet (or white)

STONE: amethyst, clear quartz crystal, diamond

SYMBOL: the thousand-petaled lotus, upward-pointing triangle inside

10 | Decoration and Design

The job of the artist is always to deepen the mystery.

——FRANCIS BACON

Imagination is a significant part of magical practice. It's the root of visualization and belief. In addition, creativity adds a personal touch to your rituals and spells. This chapter explores ways you can dress up plain candles and make special ones; create arrangements for your altar combining candles, crystals, and plants; and explore other unique ways of burning your candles. You will also discover symbols and runes you can use to carve your candles and add deeper magical significance to your work. And finally, you will begin to create your own unique candle spells.

Techniques for Decorating Candles

Now that you've mastered the art of crafting practical, magical candles, let's work on making some pretty ones!

Plain candles work, but sometimes you just want something extra special. Perhaps you want to give a magical candle as a gift or make one for a special celebration. If you simply love aesthetically pleasing candles, try some of these suggestions.

Frosting

This is a simple technique, and I frequently frost my magical candles, especially the sabbat candles. This hides any surface imperfections, and it only takes a few minutes.

This is one of the easiest ways to "dress up" a simple candle. First, save some of your molten wax and keep it hot while your candle cools (or reheat wax when you're ready to frost). When your candle is cool and out of its mold, you're ready to frost. For this technique, you'll need various brushes, such as small paint brushes or even makeup brushes. Remember that once you use these brushes for wax, they won't be good for anything else.

Dip the brush into the wax while it's still in the carafe, or pour a small amount into one of the waxed paper cups or a juice can. Then simply blot or spread it on the cooled candle. This will take some practice, but have fun and experiment to see what the results look like. You can "draw" with a small brush or, using a large brush, blot clumps of wax on the outside of the candle—this can be done to resemble snow or frost, hence the name. The wax will cool almost instantly. You can then layer it to achieve your desired effect.

You can use the same color wax as your candle, or a different color. Remember that if you do use the same color, it will look considerably lighter on the surface. A nice look for Imbolc, for example, would be to make a pale green candle and frost it with white wax. Don't forget to also frost the top of your candle, around the wick. (You don't need to worry about the bottom.)

Layering

Adding or "gluing" items to the outer surface of a candle is a fun, creative technique. This is best done with larger candles that have smaller wicks—it's important that an outer shell of wax remain while the candle is burning, preserving the decoration. You may have seen these in stores—some have shells, dried fruit, or even entire cinnamon sticks imbedded in the outer layer of candle wax. To do this, hold your finished candle by the wick and dip it into molten wax. Quickly attach the decorations to the outside while the wax is hot. If the wax dries too quickly, use a paint brush to add more hot wax to the candle's surface. An alternative method is to add flower petals or leaves on the outside of the candle with clear wax using a small paint brush. Just brush a dot of wax on the candle to adhere the fresh petal or leaf, then brush a thin layer of wax over it. The clear wax will dry, and you'll see the decoration beneath.

Fire and Ice: Ice Candles and Ice Lanterns

These are two special candles that are great for spells and rituals that pertain to the element of water.

Ice Candles

Ice candles look best in bold colors such as red, green, or dark blue. The end product will be a candle filled with holes, a kind of Swiss-cheese effect. Beware: these are tricky! You'll need some new taper candles for this project. Use a 1-quart milk carton as a mold.

- Cut away the top of the carton, making the mold whatever height you desire. Make a small hole in the bottom so the taper's wick can fit through it.

- You will need to remove enough wax from the taper so that it's the same height as the milk carton, but don't cut the wick. Expose part of the wick of the taper candle by breaking off the wax. Put the taper inside the center of the carton and push the wick through the hole—the taper candle will be the center of your finished ice candle. The bottom of the carton will be the top of the candle.

- Hold the milk carton with the wick coming through the hole at the bottom. Center the taper and fill the mold with ice cubes broken into irregular pieces (about a half inch in size), all around the taper. (Store-bought cubes work best, as they are harder.) The ice will hold the taper in place. Since the taper contains the wick, it also holds the wick.

- Put the carton in a container with a flat bottom and high sides so the water can leak out as the ice melts. (The wax is thick and will cool quickly, so it won't leak out.)

- Pour hot wax over the ice, filling the carton. Pour in a circular motion around the taper so the wax is even. As the candle cools and the ice melts, the water will seep out through the hole in the bottom of the carton, leaving holes in the wax where the ice cubes were.

- Allow the candle to cool for several hours.

- Pour off any excess water and peel away the carton. Turn it over; trim the wick. You may need to chip away some wax to form a flat bottom.

Ice Lanterns

Another "cool" technique (pun intended) is to make an ice candleholder to burn candles outside in the winter. These ice lanterns make a lovely addition to a winter party—guests can see them burning on a patio or porch.

You'll need two freezer-proof bowls. One should be fairly large, about 8 inches in diameter, and the other should be smaller, about 4 inches in diameter. Fill the large bowl with water up to about 2 inches from the edge of the bowl. Immerse the smaller bowl inside the water and put a tiny weight inside it to hold it down so the bowl rims are even. (Some water may spill over, but that's okay.) Use masking or duct tape to hold the smaller bowl in place, if necessary. Freeze until solid, at least 24 hours. To remove the ice lantern, fill a sink with hot water and submerge the mold. This will release the ice from both containers. What you have now is a bowl-shaped block of ice, perfect for holding a candle! The glow from these icy lanterns is lovely on a winter's night. Of course, the colder it is outside, the longer they will last—usually up to several hours. If the temperature outside is below freezing, they'll last much longer. If they don't melt, you can store them in a freezer or outside.

Other Magical Burning Techniques and Tips

Each candle spell or recipe in this book offers suggestions for using the candles in ritual or decorating your altar or other space. You are only limited by your imagination (and safety considerations).

Think about the type of magic you are working—for example, if the major element is water, floating candles would be ideal. A simpler method is to find a candleholder that has a "shelf" placed over a clear bowl so you can fill the bowl with water, shells, stones, etc., and burn the candle on top. You can simulate this by using a good-sized bowl and a glass candleholder: put your glass candleholder in the middle of the bowl and surround it with herbs, flowers, water, or stones. This nesting technique can be used to create lovely centerpieces for dinners and celebrations. It looks especially lovely with a glass bowl, so the items can be seen. And this way, your flowers and herbs are safe from catching fire. Be sure to use a glass candleholder that is tall enough to keep the candle safe and the flame away from your materials.

Another good combination is stones and water (earth and water) or feathers and potpourri (air and fire). Or perhaps feathers, potpourri or stones, and shells—then when you add the candle, you have a representation of each element!

Creating a display with mirrors is also a lovely way to practice candle magic. I like to burn candles in clear containers on top of mirrors to reflect the light. This is especially nice during a full moon.

Don't just toss things on your altar, arrange them! You can even do this on a table as a centerpiece or on a mantle. Most people will think it's just a lovely decorative arrangement and not even know it holds magical intent. You can display this prominently in your home or keep it private.

Make candles the center of your arrangement and decorate around them. Put flowers and herbs into vases or jars. Set stones around as accent pieces. Just use caution when placing plants near the candles—don't risk starting a fire. Small candles such as votives or tea lights in containers are usually your best bet if you plan to have a tall vase of flowers nearby, but even so, watch out for sparks! Don't leave the candle burning in the arrangement unattended.

I had just such an arrangement burning on my fireplace mantle one Winter Solstice night. There were three red taper candles arranged with pine cones and pine branches clustered at the base. My parents were over for dinner, and I could see the mantle from the dining room table. All at once we saw flames rising from it! The candles were sitting in a candleholder, but they melted all the way down, lighting the pinecones at their base on fire. Luckily, we caught it immediately and no harm was done.

It would have been much wiser in this case to use votives in tall glass jars. Needless to say, I don't use that arrangement anymore! In fact, I almost never burn taper candles, or even pillar candles. I do sometimes burn a large pillar in-side a hurricane-style container or on an open pedestal, but I always watch them carefully, never burning them for more than a couple hours at a time. One way to sidestep this problem is to place a tiny glass tea light holder in the well that is created when a larger candle burns a good way down. You can then replace the tea light inside it repeatedly, and from a distance, it looks like the original candle is burning. In fact, you can do this with any pillar or three-wick candles you are fond of in order to make them last longer.

Some Other Ideas to Try

- Use clear tea light cups whenever you can find them. I buy the bulk tea lights in metal cups but pop out the candles and place them in the plastic clear cups I've purchased with specialty candles. Or, purchase glass tea light cups. These look nicer when burning because the glow of the candle shines through the clear holder and accents the candleholder you're using. The metal holders, on the other hand, block out some of the light.

- Use mirrors to reflect candle light. Put mirrors inside bowls, add water, and float candles on top. Or, set candleholders on top of a mirror. Arrange mirrors behind your candles. This amplifies the light and is a great way to work mirror magic, especially on full moon nights.

- Arrange your candles so they light up dark corners or reflect objects such as metal or stone. I like to strategically place candles near crystal clusters so the light reflects off the stone and creates a sparkle. Place stones around the outside of your candle container.

- Use candles outside—it's a fun way to brighten up your garden or patio. Put candles on plant stands, buy hanging lanterns that hold candles, make lanterns for walkways, or even pour candles in shells. Always be sure to supervise the burning of outdoor candles!

- Pour candles into wine glasses.

- If you prefer a smooth, shiny finish, buff your finished candles with old nylon pantyhose.

- Burn candles in a container of colored sand or tiny pebbles or shells.

- Layer your candleholders. I have one lovely piece that is a lotus blossom on the outside, but inside is a glass votive cup with a pattern on it. When the candle is burning, the light shines through and marks the lotus flower petals with that pattern. It's a striking look.

- Find candleholders made of stone or crystal clusters.

- Pour wax into emptied-out (and cleaned) egg shells. Make these just like you would a votive candle, except don't remove the mold. Display them in egg cups for a creative spring decoration. You can even use yellow wax, if you'd like, to simulate egg yolks.

- Roll candles in coarsely ground spices for a rustic effect. Simply hold your candles by the wick and quickly dip them into molten wax. Set the candle on a sheet of waxed paper for a minute so the wax coating is a bit cool but still sticky. Carefully roll the candle on a cookie sheet lined with spices such as cloves, cinnamon, and nutmeg. Let it dry overnight. This technique works great with rolled beeswax taper candles (you can buy sheets of beeswax at craft stores and just follow the directions). Dip the taper candle and then roll it in the spices. You can also combine spices with dried herbs to encrust the candles.

Candles and Crystals

Since stones and crystals are often an important aspect of magic, find ways to combine them in spells and altar layouts. Earlier we discussed placing a small stone in your candle mold before pouring the wax, or burning a candle with stones around it (either inside the candleholder or outside). But there are other lovely ways to combine crystal and candle magic.

First, consider the decorative ideas mentioned earlier in this chapter. If you have lots of tumbled stones or just a few rocks you've collected, you already know they make lovely accent pieces in the home. Fill a glass dish with tumbled stones and burn a candle on top of them (put the candle inside a smaller glass holder to keep the wax off the stones).

Think about themes and color combinations that correspond to your spell and use stones along with herbs, flowers, and other plants. For example, a spell that uses sun energy or the element of fire could be complemented by amber and marigold flowers. A dish of all white or clear quartz, or a mixture of quartz and moonstones, could be combined with a white full moon candle. For a lovely winter altar display, use a green candle in a glass holder placed on a dish with pine cones, pine branches, and holly around it. For fall, use autumn leaves, acorns, and "earthy" stones such as tiger's eye. Remember to keep the candle flame safely away from plant materials; using a glass candleholder is the easiest way to do this.

You can burn a candle in a dish of sea shells and water. Or use candles to illuminate a crystal ball for scrying. Create layouts in geometric shapes around your candle using stones that correspond to your spell. The Symbols section on pages 192–94 may help you find an appropriate pattern.

To charge an item such as a piece of jewelry, a talisman, or a stone, burn a candle on top of the item. For example, if you want to charge an image with protection energy, put a protection candle in a container and place the image underneath it. If the item is an object, invert a glass dish over the item you wish to charge, then burn the candle in a separate container set on top of that. When stacking containers this way, be sure the bottom container is wide enough so that the top container won't slide off. You can also make a ring of stones or crystals around the candle. See Appendix A for a list of correspondences. Or you can simply place the item near the candle. Visualization is more important than the exact placement of the item to be charged.

Carving Candles

Some of the spells in this book mention carving a word or symbol into the candle before burning. You can extend this practice by making the act of carving part of your ritual or spell. Visualize and chant as you carve symbols or words on your candles. If you study runes, carve runes into your candles that are specific to the type of magic you are working. You can use a toothpick to carve with, but I find that using the point of a crystal feels more magical. I have one special crystal that I only use for this purpose.

Symbols are basically things that represent ideas. Simple ones include a dollar sign to represent money, or a heart to symbolize love. But symbols usually stand for something deeper and more profound than they appear, especially spiritual symbols. These symbols awaken understanding within us and suggest a complex meaning belied by their apparent simplicity. Symbols make a powerful connection with our mind—seeing a symbol that you associate with a strong feeling can add depth to your magical practice.

You know the saying "a picture is worth a thousand words." Symbols often carry deep connotations, or messages that we understand instantly by seeing the item or object and connecting it with all our cultural and personal associations. This is one reason that not all symbolic meaning is shared in the same way by everyone.

Symbols can be more than abstract drawings or images. Symbols can be complex geometric designs, such as mandalas (a Hindu/Buddhist geometric symbol that represent the universe) or any of a number of religious symbols. Natural objects are often used as symbols, such as animals, trees, and flowers (remember the discussion of the classical elements in Chapter 5). Other symbols are jewelry (rings are popular symbols for rites of passages such as graduation and marriage) and emblems such as flags and coats of arms. Obviously, candles are symbols themselves, representing the element of fire, the light of the sun, spirituality, transformation, and so on.

While similar symbols can have different meanings across cultures, some scholars believe that certain symbols transcend culture—that there are some symbols that are understood by everyone. Psychologist Carl Jung referred to these when he discussed the "collective unconscious"—the belief that experiences and memories of our ancestors can somehow still resonate with us, no matter our heritage. He called these similar images "archetypes," and some of the most popular ones are the "anima" and "animus." These are the female and male principles, respectively, that conjure up specific ideals such as goddess, queen, princess, sorceress, god, king, wizard, prince, hero, and so on. These are powerful personalities that are known across time and cultures. Many of them appear in the Tarot. Consider making use of these archetypes when working with deities and symbols.

Symbols can mean different things to different people, but they often contain similar meaning within a culture. For example, to most Americans, a bird might represent freedom (such as our national symbol, the eagle) and a tree symbolizes nature, grounding, and connection with the earth. To nearly everyone, the rose symbolizes love. To decide on a symbol, base your decision on the first impulse you have, your first reaction to the item—what does it suggest to you? You may have a personal feeling about something that differs from popular perception, based on a personal experience. Ask yourself how a symbol makes you feel. What associations do you connect with it? Use symbols that resonate with you and explore the meaning behind those that are new to you. In addition, you may create and use personal symbols of your own, making them especially relevant to your purpose.

Air

Ankh

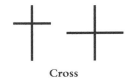

Crescent moon

Cross

Fire

Moon with crescent on top

Pentacle, earth

Solomon's Seal

Spiral

Sun

Triple moon

Triskele

Water

Yin and yang

Symbols

Below are some symbols commonly used in magic and spiritual practice. There are also symbols used to represent all the planets and the signs of the zodiac. See Chapter 7 for more information.

AIR: The element of air.

ANKH: Ancient Egyptian symbol for eternal life.

CRESCENT MOON: Lunar associations, feminine qualities, intuition.

CROSS: The cross, in various forms, has been used by many cultures throughout history—the Native Americans used a cross with equal sides to represent the four directions, and the cross is a sacred symbol to Christians. In fact, Constantine, in an effort to find a religion that would unite the Roman Empire, favored the cross symbol because it was the holy symbol of the Christians and also represented the four quarters of Earth.

FIRE: The element of fire.

MOON WITH CRESCENT ON TOP: The horned god of nature.

PENTACLE: Protection, earth element.

SOLOMON'S SEAL OR STAR OF DAVID: The Jewish faith uses this symbol of two triangles, which represents the balance of the universe. This was also a symbol of Pythagorean philosophy: each triangle is composed of nine points, which was considered to be a sacred number, and when they overlap and a point in the center is added, the total is thirteen points—another special number.

SPIRAL: Energy, sun, eternal life, nature, rebirth.

SUN: Solar associations, masculine energy, strength.

TRIPLE MOON: The aspects of the goddess.

TRISKELE (TRIPLE KNOT): Protection.

WATER: To represent the element of water.

YIN AND YANG: Chinese symbol that represents the union of opposites—female and male.

Runes

Since the first human used a stick to draw in the dirt, people have been creating figures and symbols to communicate. Cave paintings, pictographs, and other ancient forms of writing have been found all over the world. Runes like the ones depicted here are often composed of straight lines because they were traditionally carved or burned into wood or bone, or chiseled into stone or metal.

The runes referred to in this book come from an alphabet called the Elder Futhark (containing twenty-four runes), which originated with ancient Germanic tribes. The names come from various sources—trees, animals, gods, and other objects or concepts.

Runes are not a language that can be exactly translated into modern English. A reference book on runes will contain equivalent letters and sounds if you are interested, but for magical use, being familiar with a few runes and their meanings can be useful. To fully immerse yourself in the study of runes is one of many paths magical practice can take. Runes are typically used in divination, but you can draw on the influence of runic symbolism in candle magic.

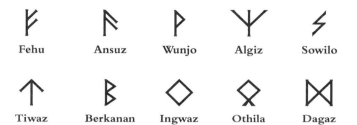

Fehu Ansuz Wunjo Algiz Sowilo

Tiwaz Berkanan Ingwaz Othila Dagaz

Here are some correspondences for ten of these runes. I have selected these ten because I believe them to be the most useful for candle magic. The study of runes is complex and rewarding. If this interests you, I encourage you to continue studying the runic mysteries.

FEHU: Carve this symbol into candles for wealth, fulfillment, and abundance. Associated with the elements of fire and earth and the goddess Freya.

ANSUZ: Carve this rune into candles for knowledge, leadership, wisdom, and communication. Also used for prophecy and revelation. Associated with the element of air and the god Odin.

WUNJO: Use for joy, happiness, and harmony. Associated with the element of water, the god Odin, and the goddess Frigg.

ALGIZ: A rune that represents opportunity for growth, protection, and success. Associated with the element of air and masculine energy.

SOWILO: This rune represents the sun. Use for energy, light, discovery, and strength. Masculine energy.

TIWAZ: Use for protection and courage. Also determination, male sexuality, and compassion. Named for the Norse warrior god Tiw and associated with the element of air. Astrological correspondence is Libra.

BERKANAN: Use for growth and fertility. Also new beginnings, healing, and purification. Associated with the element of earth and feminine energy.

INGWAZ: This is the rune of peace and harmony. Use for love and unity. Associated with the elements of earth and water, named for the Norse hero-god Ing, and associated with the new moon.

OTHILA: Use this rune for issues that relate to the family, home, possessions, and other domestic issues. Masculine energy, associated with the element of earth and the god Odin. Astrological correspondence is the full moon.

DAGAZ: This is the rune of transformation and change. *Dagaz* means "day" and is associated with the light of dawn, or a new day. Associated with the elements of fire and air. Use during the waxing or waning moon phase.

Group Candle Work

It's fun to make candles with your coven, if you happen to be part of one. Since molten wax will hold its heat for a while, you can remove the carafe of wax and place it on a table (don't forget to use a hot pad). Then everyone can gather around the "cauldron" and the group can energize the wax as part of a ritual. After the candles are poured and hardened, everyone in the group can have a candle that is empowered with the group's energy. (Pour the candles at the beginning of the gathering to allow them time to cool and harden enough to move. They can be removed from their molds the following day.) These candles can be burned as part of a remote spell or ritual if the group can't be together physically, or each person can use their candle for whatever they need, adding the power of the group to their personal magic. Alternatively, you can pour the candles in advance for everyone in your group and then charge them together.

Group-made candles can be used for anything—they are especially good for initiation and degree ceremonies, group affirmation and release rituals, and other rites of passage.

Create Your Own Candle Spells

I hope that you have enjoyed this journey through candle crafting, as well as learning about magic and how to use it while creating special candles. Always remember that your intent is the key to successful and rewarding magic. Now that you've practiced, it's time to take the next step and write your own spells and recipes for magical candles! You can use the candle spells in this book as a guide, or use the following template. You might want to make photocopies of the template for creating multiple spells. If you have a Book of Shadows, you might consider pasting your spells inside it and decorating them appropriately.

Once you've answered the questions, use the information—along with correspondences for days of the week, color, and moon phase—to help you create your own spells. Chapter 7 contains information on planetary and astrological correspondences. See Chapter 4 for days of the week and Chapter 5 for elemental correspondences. Days, planets, signs, and seasons each have a different influence, and these can be combined in a variety of ways; this is one reason magic is so creative and should be personalized for each individual practitioner.

Look over your list and decide which correspondences are most important to you. Moon phase should take top priority, along with moon sign, color, and energy style. However, your need will be based on your current situation and the accessibility of ingredients.

Magic is not rigid. You are never locked in to only one way or time to work magic. Correspondences are simply suggestions and guidelines designed to help you focus and take advantage of elemental energy. Don't forget that the source of magic is within you. Remember, all things are connected, and that's where the magic is—in your relationship with the world around you, what you believe and honor, and how you live.

Candle Spell for _____

Written by:

What is your goal? What do you want or need? Include as much detail as possible.

Is the energy style receptive—drawing something to yourself or manifesting something? Or is it projective—sending something out into the universe or transforming yourself?

What color or colors would be the best choice for this spell? *(Chapter 2)*

List the days of the week to make and burn this spell candle. *(Chapter 4)*

Which element best describes this spell? List the characteristics here. *(Chapter 5)*

Photocopy this form for creating your own spell candles.

What would be the best moon phase for this spell? Consider new, waxing, full, waning, and dark moon phases. *(Chapter 7)*

Which moon sign or signs best describe your intention? *(Chapter 7)*

Which numbers best represent the purpose of this spell candle? How else can numbers be used in this spell? *(Appendix A)*

List any appropriate ingredients, such as herbs, essential oils, and stones. *(Chapter 3 and Appendix A)*

Are there any gods or goddesses that seem particularly well suited to this spell? *(Appendix A)*

Write a chant. Use what I call the three Rs of chant writing: Rhyme, Rhythm, and Repetition. Keep your words simple, yet meaningful. Make sure the words flow well and are easy to repeat and remember.

Photocopy this form for creating your own spell candles.

You Are the Magic: Defining Your Personal Practice

The unexamined life is not worth living.

—SOCRATES

I would like to conclude this book with a personal message. If you're reading this, you are a seeker. I hope that no matter what spiritual path you follow, you follow it truly and with open eyes. Continue to learn and seek and know fully why you hold the beliefs you do. Immerse yourself in them. Don't just believe what someone has told you; experience it and understand.

Human history is filled with changes brought about by people in search of answers. Eastern philosophy introduced us to teachings about peace, impermanence, and change. The ancients of the West—great Greek philosophers Socrates, Plato, and Aristotle—taught us to question everything, to examine the true essence of things through critical thinking, logic, and temperance. (The Golden Mean Aristotle spoke of is a kind of balance.) But then something happened in the West. There was a period of strict religious dogma when no one was allowed to question anything. Faith and doubt were at war. Luckily, that period didn't last, and the Reformation and the Scientific Revolution gave us new insight. In the words of Francis Bacon, "knowledge is power," and so progress was made. But that progress came with a price. We learned about science and perspective, but we forgot something else. The Romantics reminded us that technology doesn't necessarily mean happiness. They revived emotion, spirituality, and art. The Industrial Revolution didn't improve life for everyone—the Existentialists remind us of that. Throughout history, people have sought answers and new experiences, and it seems as though science and religion have been tugging people back and forth, forcing them to choose sides.

There's still so much we don't know about life and our world. This is where mysticism resides. Science has given us wonderful knowledge and advancements, but it has also driven many away from spirituality, or reduced people to empty rituals and routines. The scholar Anthony Aveni wrote about this loss: "We need to be aware of what we lost when we unglued the bond between matter and spirit and traded away the animated half of the world for the limited free will we have exercised so briefly to probe the other half of existence….We have depersonalized Mother Nature…but we are beginning to pay the price of living in a motherless world."

While Aveni wasn't writing specifically about magic, his words ring true for magical practitioners. I think a philosophical and magical frame of mind can help us reconnect with what we have lost. We can feel the awe of what science shows us along with the awe of the unknown. The more we continue to seek, the more questions—deeper questions—will lead us on our journey. And it's more than just asking questions, but asking the *right* questions. Knowing what you believe and why and defining your self will give you strength that can deepen your spiritual experience and your magic.

Learn from mystics and scholars, scientists, and poets—and from yourself. Combine reason with personal revelation. Can you reconcile a belief in both science and magic? Absolutely. Look to the ancient mystics for inspiration, as their words still ring true. Study philosophy and history. Observe the world around you. My own spiritual beliefs are often reaffirmed by science. Much of what we take for granted today as knowledge would have been considered magic to people who lived thousands of years ago. Some people say magic is just science that hasn't been explained yet. Maybe. Until such a time, keep an open mind. Question everything, but also keep a sense of adventure.

Remember that all things are connected. Find your passion and pursue it relentlessly. As mythologist Joseph Campbell is famous for saying, "Follow your bliss." This means so much more than it seems. More than just doing what you like, it means living your path to the fullest. If you are on the right path, the way will be clear. If you practice the magical arts, do so in depth. Magic as a hobby is rarely effective. True magic is a lifestyle. Knowing why you believe what you believe makes your convictions stronger, and it creates a deeper sense of understanding and connection.

Magic is energy, the power of life itself. It is sacred. It permeates all things. And I can't imagine a more perfect symbol than light to represent this magical spark of life and enlightenment. Candles have long been a symbol of illumination—of the spirit and of the mind. Let this light be your guide.

| # Correspondences

Herbs, Oils, Resins, and Woods

Basil *Ocimum basilicum*

MASCULINE, MARS, FIRE

Love, exorcism, wealth, protection, divination, good luck for a new home. Basil promotes love and prosperity. It sharpens the conscious mind and brings happiness and peace. Often used in money spells. Use the dried leaves. Basil is a long-standing Witch's herb used for a variety of magical purposes.

Cedar/Juniper

MASCULINE, SUN, FIRE

Cedar (cedarwood) oil is more common in magic than the actual wood from the tree. Healing, protection, purification. Cedar actually belongs to the pine family. There are four species of cedar trees that are considered "true cedar" and these are native to North Africa, Cyprus, Lebanon, Syria, and Turkey. The cedar trees we are most familiar with in North America are actually *Juniperus virginiana* (Eastern Red Cedar) or *Thuja occidentalis* (Eastern White Cedar)—both junipers. The essential oil I have been using is called Texas Cedarwood and it is *Juniperus mexicana*. Just look for cedarwood essential oil and don't be concerned about which tree it's from. We can apply the properties of cedar as corresponding to the "cedar" trees we know.

The smoke of burning cedar is purifying. Native Americans burned it for purification and ceremonial fires. *Cedar* is a Semitic word that means "the power of spiritual strength," referring to the species of tree native to Morocco, Lebanon, and other places in the Far East. The oil is extracted from the wood; this is believed by some to be one of the earliest-known oils. The essential oil aroma has an uplifting effect that can boost confidence and overcome fears. The aroma also helps eliminate mental stagnation. It's relaxing and soothing—use to aid meditation and promote spirituality. It's calming, and helps bring oneself into balance. Cedar oil should be avoided by pregnant women.

Chamomile *Chamaemelum nobile*

FEMININE, VENUS, WATER

Chamomile has a feminine quality and is associated with Venus and the element of water. Use for spells involving sleep, love, purification, meditation, money, and protection. To remove spells cast against you, sprinkle chamomile around your property. The flowers are associated with the sun due to their appearance.

You can simply buy chamomile tea and break open a tea bag for finely ground flowers. Chamomile essential oil can also be used. This plant was revered by the ancient Egyptians as sacred to the sun. Chamomile was said to be used in Midsummer Eve bonfires (along with other herbs). There are several varieties, but Roman and German are the most common—they have similar properties but different appearance.

Cinnamon (dried, powdered) *Cinnamomum zeylanicum*

MASCULINE, SUN, FIRE

Some sources attribute cinnamon to Venus and Aphrodite, lending it power for use in love and prosperity spells. You can burn ground cinnamon as incense or use it in sachets for spirituality, healing, attracting money, stimulating psychic powers, and protection.

Use caution with essential oil on the skin. Recipes in this book only use the powdered form, not the oil.

Clove *Syzygium aromaticum* or *Caryophyllus aromaticus*

MASCULINE, JUPITER, FIRE

Protection, exorcism, love, healing, money, memory, courage. Burn whole cloves as incense to attract riches, drive away negativity, promote spirituality, and purify a space. Carry them mixed with cinnamon to attract the opposite sex. Cloves can also be used to comfort and relieve grief. This is a good herb to use to draw the positive and achieve balance by driving away the negative. Promotes a sense of home and family connections.

Recipes in this book only use the powdered or whole cloves, not the oil. The oil is very irritating to the skin.

Dill *Anethum graveolens*

MASCULINE, MERCURY, FIRE AND AIR

Protection (especially against magic), money, lust, love—add to a bath to become irresistible. Cleansing and purification. Sharpens the mind. It has a calming quality and a cleansing aroma. This book uses only the plant, not the oil.

Frankincense *Boswellia thurifera*

MASCULINE, SUN, FIRE AND AIR

With 3,000 years of continuous usage, frankincense, one of the oldest magical incenses, comes from the gum of a small tree that grows in the Middle East. Most well-known for its Biblical references, the old French name *franc encens* means "luxuriant." It's often used as incense for meditation, purification, cleansing, spirituality, and consecration of ritual tools. Carry the resin "tears" for protection. The oil is also used in magic.

The aroma of frankincense is one of the most recognizable scents, often burned in churches and temples. It is uplifting, rejuvenating, inspiring, and contemplative. Regulating yet stimulating, it relieves exhaustion and mental fatigue. Boosts confidence; aids meditation. It produces heightened awareness of spiritual realms, deepens religious experience, and reduces stress and tension.

Geranium *Pelargonium*
FEMININE, VENUS, WATER

Fertility, health, love, protection. Women use this to heighten romance. The oil comes from "rose geranium" and is thought to keep evil spirits at bay. Its energy is balancing, harmonizing, cleansing, stimulating, and uplifting. Protects against psychic attack; helps manifest a goal.

Ginger *Zingiber officinale*
MASCULINE, MARS, FIRE

Magical energy, physical energy, sex, love, money, courage. Inhale the aroma during visualization, but don't breathe too much before bedtime—it may keep you awake.

Native to south Asia, ginger is warm and comforting, balancing and grounding. The oil comes from the root, and eating the root is said to aid digestion and nausea. It warms the emotions, sharpens the senses, and aids memory. You can use both the root and the oil. Ginger was once worth more than its weight in gold!

Jasmine *Jasminum officinale*

FEMININE, MOON, WATER

Jasmine is a renowned aphrodisiac, often used in love potions. It's also a popular ingredient in tea and has some medicinal uses. However, it can cause headaches in some people. Jasmine is emotionally warming, unites opposing factors within us, and is useful to get rid of apathy or indifference. Also used for peace, spirituality, sex, sleep, and psychic dreams. Jasmine oil is very, very expensive, but it's worth having if you can afford it—use it sparingly and make it last. Jasmine is often called the king of flowers (rose is the queen).

Lavender *Lavandula officinalis/angustifolia*

MASCULINE, MERCURY, AIR

Use for spiritual love, protection, sleep, chastity/celibacy, health, longevity, purification, conscious mind, happiness, and peace. Use in sachets or make an infusion for cleaning or bathing to create peace and restfulness. Burn with sandalwood to attract helpful spirits. Lavender is gently sedative and balancing; alleviates panic, impatience, and anger; can help relieve headaches; cleanses physically and spiritually; helps break bad habits; and is soothing during a crisis. Lavender can be used to change the way one thinks about love.

Lavender symbolizes silence and attracts love. It is also a symbol of affection. Can be used for relaxation and relieving stress and headaches; the calming scent is also gently reviving.

Marigold *Calendula officinalis*

MASCULINE, SUN, FIRE

Protection, prophetic dreams, legal matters, psychic powers. Carry with you for justice in court. Look at marigolds to strengthen sight. Believed to drive away evil and evil thoughts.

These flowers have strong ties with Indian and Arabic cultures. They were used to decorate temples and shrines, statues of gods, and funerals. They are symbolic of life, eternity, and health. Greek legend says this flower grew in a spot where a maiden who loved the sun god watched for him every morning at sunrise. The girl eventually wasted away, so absorbed by her passion—this flower grew in the place where she waited.

Mint *Mentha*

MASCULINE, MERCURY, AIR

Use in spells for money, lust, healing, travel, exorcism, and protection. Dried mint doesn't smell particularly good when burned, so use the oil for aromatherapy.

Myrrh *Comniphora myrrha*

FEMININE, MOON AND SATURN, WATER

Similar to frankincense, the resin and oil are both used. Used for spirituality, meditation, and healing. Myrrh has been used in magic and religion for at least 4,000 years (commonly paired with frankincense). Use to awaken spirituality.

Oak *Quercus alba*

MASCULINE, SUN, FIRE

Protection, health, money, healing, potency, fertility, luck. Many types of trees have been associated with magical practice or considered sacred. If you have oak trees in your yard, you know what wonderful trees they are. In magical practice, the leaves are often used, and sometimes the acorns and branches. The oak has been worshipped throughout history, and it provided food for early people. Believed to be sacred to the Druids, the oak is a long-lived tree, strong and sturdy. Use acorn magic to cause sudden change.

Orange *Citrus aurantia*

MASCULINE, SUN, FIRE

Use for purification, joy, physical energy, and magical energy. The oil comes from a smaller fruit, the Seville orange, which is not the one we commonly eat. This plant has long been a symbol of both innocence and fertility. The oil does not keep very long. It is mellow, warming, soothing, creates a positive outlook and cheerfulness, and also revives the spirit.

Parsley *Petroselinum crispum, P. sativum*

MASCULINE, MERCURY, AIR

Use for protection, purification, lust, and fertility. Parsley has long been used in folk medicine—it was mentioned by the Greeks in the third century BC. They used it in wedding ceremonies and believed it attracted peace and tranquility. Parsley is also associated with death—specifically the goddess Persephone. Parsley was used to decorate tombs and was believed to help guide souls on their passage to the afterlife. The Romans believed it increased stamina and so ate it before battles. It was rumored to only flourish in homes where the woman was master of the house and was believed unlucky to transplant or give away. Some people believed only a Witch could grow it successfully. The fresh herb is aromatic, but use it dried in molten candle wax.

Peppermint Mentha piperita

MASCULINE, MERCURY, FIRE

Peppermint oil is a good one to have around for magic, and it's not very expensive. It dispels negative thoughts and can be used for purification. Use to remedy mental fatigue; aids clear thinking and helps with anger, nervousness, and shyness. Can be irritant on the skin. May disturb sleep patterns if inhaled too often before bedtime.

Legend says this herb was created when Hades was dazzled by the beauty of a nymph called Minthe. Persephone, Hades's wife, was jealous and so changed the nymph into a plant. Mint has long been used in magic and sorcery—a sprig of mint on the altar is said to aid all magical workings. Remains of mint have been found in Egyptian tombs as far back as 1000 BC. It was used by the ancient Egyptians, Chinese, and Indians and was believed by some to be an aphrodisiac; it increases vitality.

Pine *Pinus*

MASCULINE, MARS, AIR

Use for spells involving healing, fertility (the cones), protection, exorcism, and money. If you're lucky enough to have pine trees in your yard, you can use the needles and cones in magic. You can burn the needles as incense to purify and cleanse or to reverse spells. According to folklore, put branches over the bed for health or to drive away illness. Eat pine nuts before projective (masculine) magic to cause sudden change or while working with air and fire elements.

Pine Essential Oil: Healing, purification, protection, physical energy, magical energy, money. Pine essential oil is one of the more affordable oils to work with.

Rose *Rosa*

FEMININE, VENUS, WATER

Love, psychic powers, healing, love divination, luck, protection. Use red and pink petals in sachets and incense to draw love.

Rose Oil (Rosa damascene/Rosa centifolia): Relieves loneliness, grief, and past emotional trauma. Aids relationships, calms bitter feelings of jealousy or anger, and helps with fresh starts, healing, and cleansing. Love, peace, sex, beauty.

Rosemary *Rosmarinus officinalis*

MASCULINE, SUN, FIRE

Associated with protection, love, lust, mental powers, exorcism, purification, healing, and youth. Rosemary essential oil is commonly used in magic. The ancient Romans decorated with it to honor the gods. It was also commonly burned—the smoke is purifying. Rosemary oil on the forehead is said to strengthen memory. Its name is derived from the Latin *Ros-marinus*, "dew of the sea," due to its growth in coastal regions. Rosemary is also an herb of the sun and is used in spells to increase vitality. It's used for both weddings and funerals due to its associations with love and remembrance. It can also be used to dispel nightmares. It was used in the Middle Ages to drive away evil spirits (most likely due to its disinfectant properties). Rosemary essential oil has a stimulating aroma that relieves fatigue and strengthens an exhausted mind.

Wash your hands with rosemary before doing healing work. Combine it with sage for smudging. Rosemary is associated with the Maiden aspect of the Triple Goddess. It can be used as a psychic protector for individuals and places. It can also be used to stimulate love and in spells for longevity, to clear the mind, and to aid memory.

Sage *Salvia officinalis*
MASCULINE, JUPITER, AIR

Associated with immortality, longevity, strength, wisdom, protection, and wishes. Also used in healing and money spells and for memory and the conscious mind. Can be used in spells for love and fertility. Sage eases grief and is used for remembrance. Expels evil spirits. Use the plant only; sage oil is dangerous and should not be used.

Ancient cultures have long considered sage to have very potent magical powers. The Greeks believed it could make someone immortal, and the Egyptians regarded it as a giver and saver of lives. The Romans liked it so much that they had special rituals for harvesting it. The name *sage* comes from the Latin *salvare*, "to heal." *Salvia* means "good health." Like some other magical herbs, there is a legend that it could only flourish in a garden if the wife ruled the household. This is sometimes used as an essential oil, but that will not be needed for the spells in this book.

Sandalwood *Santalum album*
FEMININE, MOON, WATER

Often used to make protective beads. Good for creative visualization and meditation. Both the wood and essential oil are used, but the oil is more expensive.

Sandalwood has a sensuous aroma and is one of the oldest-known scented materials—it has enjoyed as many as four thousand years of uninterrupted use. The oil is distilled from the wood. The powdered wood is one of the most popular ingredients used in incense. It's expensive because it comes from the heartwood of 30-to-60-year-old trees in India that are protected by the Indian government. The aroma is gentle and sedative, encourages self-expression, and boosts confidence, peace, and acceptance. Sandalwood is useful for grieving, to release the past, to find balance and forgiveness, to aid meditation, to quiet the mind, and for healing and self-healing. It's also said to be an aphrodisiac.

Thyme *Thymus vulgaris*
FEMININE, VENUS, WATER

Use for health, healing, sleep, psychic powers, love and lust, purification, courage, and energy. Thyme oil is somewhat toxic and is not used.

Thyme was ritually burned as incense on altars to the gods of Greece and Rome. The herb was said to represent strength and bravery—ladies gave thyme to knights to carry into battle during the Middle Ages. Like rosemary, thyme is also associated with love and remembrance. An herb of both emotion and action, it is sacred to Venus and Mars. Folklore says eating thyme gives one the ability to see fairies. Good to use in love spells and to aid pleasant dreams and prevent nightmares (use just a small amount—thyme is a stimulating herb, so it may prevent sleep in some individuals).

Stones and Crystals

This is a very brief selection of the thousands of different types of stones and minerals used in magic. These are relatively easy to find and not very expensive, depending on the size and quality of the specimen. See the suggestions in Chapter 10 for combining stones and crystals with candle magic.

AMBER (fossilized tree resin): positive energy; healing; associated with the sun and element of earth; sensual; said to make the wearer irresistible

AMETHYST (purple quartz): promotes sobriety; helps break addictions; used for spirituality and peace and to aid sleep, transformation, and meditation

AVENTURINE (green quartz, often with flecks of mica): prosperity, a "gambler's talisman," balances male/female energies; general healing stone; increases opportunity and motivation, creativity/individuality; stress relief

CITRINE (yellow-orange-brown quartz): a stone of optimism; never needs cleansing—does not hold negative energy but dissipates and transmutes it; "the merchant's stone," good for education, business, mental clarity; teaches prosperity; promotes a sense of community; dispels fear; opens communication/positive influence

FLUORITE: promotes order and reason; concentration; meditation; "stone of discernment and aptitude"; stabilizing; helps one reach height of mental achievement, "the genius stone"

Blue: calm energy, orderly communication

Clear: aligns/cleanses aura

Green: clears negativity from a room, tidying, "minty fresh"

Purple: psychic/spiritual growth and intuition

Yellow: creativity, intellectual pursuits

GARNET: a "stone of health," promotes self-confidence, sexuality, vigor, and patience; protects against thieves; sleep with to remember dreams; also a "stone of commitment"; a variety called Grossular Garnet strengthens stability in lawsuits and legal matters

HEMATITE: purifies and balances; a "stone of the mind"; encourages self-control, grounding, and psychic awareness; transforms negativity; aids manual dexterity

LAPIS LAZULI: a "stone of total awareness"; amplifies spiritual and psychic awareness; promotes good judgment and wisdom; cheerful; stimulates creativity, mental clarity, speech, sincerity, and self-acceptance; boosts the immune system

MALACHITE: transformation; clears the path to a goal; protection (especially aviation); business prosperity; soothing and calming; anti-depressant; amplifies mood

MOONSTONE: feminine and lunar energy; "the traveler's stone"; used for cycles/changes, new beginnings; promotes intuition and insight; healing for women; heightens psychic sensitivity; calming and balancing; introspective and reflective; allows one to distinguish between needs and desires

OBSIDIAN: protective (especially from psychic vampires) and grounding; scrying; absorbs negativity; goddess mysteries; detachment with wisdom and love

Snowflake Obsidian: sharpens external and internal vision; reveals contrasts of life to realize unnecessary patterns; serenity in isolation and meditation; "stone of purity"

PYRITE (fool's gold)**:** shields from negative energy; protective; encourages health; enhances memory and understanding; practical; strengthens will and positive outlook

QUARTZ: if you can only buy one stone, this is the one to have. Suitable for all purposes, it also magnifies the energy of other stones and can be used to help direct energy. Clear quartz points are a favorite stone for the tips of wands and to help focus the mind in meditation. Use for balance, purity, meditation; amplifies energy and thoughts; promotes clarity and harmony; a "stone of power"; used for communication on all levels; spirituality, healing, energy, protection; meditation.

Clear Quartz: magnifier, all-around healer and amplifier, focus

Rose Quartz (pink): promotes self-love, clarity of emotions, forgiveness, love of others, universal love, and compassion; beautifies skin; fertility; sex; cools temper

Smoky Quartz (gray/brown to black): transforms negativity; removes emotional blocks and mental barriers; adds clarity to meditation; balances and grounds; a "stone of cooperation"; enhances personal pride and joy in life; enables one to let go; increases love of physical body; activates base chakras

SALT: plain table salt or coarse sea salt are both commonly used in magic; salt is reputed to be protective, and practitioners sometimes use salt water to purify sacred space; salt is also sometimes used to represent the element of earth

TIGER'S EYE: focus and concentration; grounding; wealth and money talisman; protection; psychic sight and insight; courage and strength; optimism—helps one to see things in the best light; slight masculine energy; balancing; enhances creativity; integrity; personal power; helps one manifest ideas into reality; blue variety is used for peace and healing, red for protection

TURQUOISE: spiritual attunement; vision quests; protection; grounding; wisdom; kindness; guidance; clarity in communication; self-awareness; helps one find one's "true purpose"

Numbers

Numerology is a fascinating field of study on its own, and it has often been deemed important in magic. You can use numbers when deciding how many candles to include in an arrangement, how many drops of an oil to use (if you don't have a specific recipe), and so on. In general, odd numbers are used for expansion and change, creativity, inspiration, and new experiences; even numbers are for stability and structure, or to make something long-lasting in your life.

If working with numbers appeals to you, research sacred geometry. This area of study focuses on the use of patterns and shapes that have been used throughout history in temples and other religious buildings, artifacts, and even musical arrangements. Certain numerical sequences are also found in nature; these ordered patterns make the study of numbers fascinating.

1: divine spark, self expression, ambition, courage, unity, roots, beginnings, masculine energy (the sun)

2: unconscious mind, duality of humanity and the Divine, emotions, harmony, cooperation, wealth, mystery, money, marriage, reflection, polarity, duality, balance, feminine energy (the moon)

3: manifestation, trinity, creativity, joy, synthesis, expansion (Jupiter)

4: earth energy, the four elements, discipline, solidarity, crossroads, will (Uranus)

5: humanity, protection, strength, intelligence, the five senses, freedom, communication (Mercury)

6: beauty, union of conscious and unconscious minds, balance, creation, perfection, healing, love, wisdom, release, union of opposites, responsibility (Venus)

7: perfect order, a mystical and sacred number, higher learning, spirituality (Neptune)

8: strength, life-force energy, discipline, eternity, authority, regeneration, courage (Saturn)

9: completeness, action, culmination, physical prowess (Mars)

10: perfection through completeness, return to unity, transformation, a plateau

11: new beginnings, higher level of understanding

12: cosmic order and perfection

Deities

I have not included specific recipes for candles made to honor a god or goddess simply because there are so many to choose from! If you would like to create candles to honor a deity, here is a brief list of some of the correspondences to get you started. This list only includes major figures from the pantheons of ancient Egyptian, Greek, Roman, Celtic, and Norse cultures. I encourage you to explore mythology to find those that resonate with you on a personal level. Reading the stories of mythology helps people gain insight into the universal truths of humanity, and it's interesting to see the parallels in myths across various cultures. Plus, the more you read and study the stories of these myths, the more each deity will come to life for you and enable you to make a personal connection. Just because these deities are no longer worshipped by large groups of people as they once were doesn't mean they are gone. Belief brings them to life.

I have paired the Greek and Roman gods and goddesses together, as they became identified with each other over time. Note that in the early day of the Roman civilization, their deities had separate identities and were not exact counterparts to Greek deities, as they sometimes appear to be.

Goddesses

APHRODITE (GREEK) AND VENUS (ROMAN): Goddess of love and beauty; also affection, renewal, and partnerships. Sometimes associated with birds such as the swan and dove. Venus was originally goddess of fruit trees and gardens.

Love Magic: element of water, pink, cinnamon, myrtle, pine and rose, frankincense and myrrh, Friday

ARTEMIS (GREEK) AND DIANA (ROMAN): Virgin goddess of the wild and the hunt; later, the identity of Artemis was merged with Selene, so Artemis became associated with the moon—however, in the Triple Goddess aspect, she represents the Maiden (New Moon/Waxing Crescent). Artemis is the twin sister of Apollo.

Protection and Healing Magic: all elements, white, silver, acorns, wormwood, clove, basil, frankincense, rosemary, Sunday

ATHENA (GREEK): Virgin goddess of wisdom, crafts, justice, and peace. Often associated with owls and snakes.

Creativity Magic: all elements, yellow, lavender, Wednesday

Strength Magic: earth element, red, frankincense, cinnamon, oak, olive, Sunday and Tuesday

BRIGID OR BRIGIT (CELTIC): Goddess of healing and fertility—also known as goddess of smithcraft and poetry—worshipped in Ireland and Britain. Also associated with prophecy, all feminine arts, love, and occult knowledge.

Creativity Magic: all elements, yellow, lavender, Wednesday

Healing Magic: all elements, frankincense, sandalwood, blue, white, Sunday, Monday

Fertility Magic: earth and water elements, green, red, geranium, pine, Monday and Sunday

CERRIDWEN (CELTIC): Welsh goddess of fertility and cycles of birth/death/ rebirth, often associated with a cauldron. Divination, herbs, and knowledge.

Creativity Magic: all elements, yellow, lavender, Wednesday

Healing Magic: all elements, frankincense, sandalwood, blue, white, Sunday and Monday

Abundance Magic: rose, element of earth, green, gold, purple, silver, basil, cinnamon, dill, Thursday and Sunday

CYBELE (GREEK AND ROMAN): Mother goddess and goddess of fertility who originated in Asia Minor (Phrygian myth), worshipped by Greeks and Romans. An earth goddess who ruled over the wild, especially in mountains, caves and other rocky areas.

Fertility Magic: earth and water elements, green, red, geranium, pine, Monday and Sunday

DEMETER (GREEK) AND CERES (ROMAN): Goddess of vegetation and fruitfulness, especially associated with corn; powers of growth and resurrection. *Demeter* means "Mother Earth." When her daughter, Persephone, was taken by Hades to be his bride in the underworld, Demeter was so distraught that Zeus allowed Persephone to return for half the year; the half she spent with Hades became the dark half of the year—this is the myth used to explain the season of winter. Demeter is often represented as the Mother (full moon) aspect of the Triple Goddess.

Abundance Magic: rose, element of earth, green, gold, purple, silver, basil, cinnamon, dill, Thursday and Sunday

FREYJA (NORSE): An important Norse fertility goddess and a sorceress.

FRIGG OR FRIGGA (NORSE): Wife of Odin. Our day Friday is named for her—a Norse fertility goddess having much in common with Freya. Cleverness and wisdom, marriage, a shape-shifter; knower of all things. Perhaps the origin of both of these was Frea, an early Germanic goddess.

Fertility Magic: earth and water elements, green, red, geranium, pine, Monday and Sunday

HECATE (GREEK): A goddess with two aspects—fertility by day and Witchcraft and ghosts by night—she combined the cycles of life as powers of Earth. Her home was in the underworld. She is a goddess of roads in general and specifically crossroads. She is often portrayed with three faces—

also used to represent the Crone aspect of the Triple Goddess (waning crescent moon) and often depicted with dogs.

Magic for balance, protection, transformation, purification, choices, exploring, breaking illusions, seeing painful truths: waning moon, mint, oak

HERA (GREEK) AND JUNO (ROMAN): Goddess called queen of the sky; wife of Zeus/Jupiter—a powerful mother goddess. She is often associated with birth, protector of marriage, and the home. *Juno* means "youth" and she was not originally the wife of Jupiter. She was a goddess of strength and vitality.

Abundance Magic: rose, element of earth, green, gold, purple, silver, basil, cinnamon, dill, willow, Thursday and Sunday

ISIS (EGYPTIAN): Mother goddess, associated with birds, the underworld, and water. Her following spread to Greece and Rome. A powerful sorceress.

Protection Magic: all elements, white, silver, clove, basil, frankincense, rosemary, Sunday

Love Magic: element of water, pink, cinnamon, pine and rose, Friday

Fertility Magic: earth and water elements, green, red, geranium, pine, Monday and Sunday

Healing Magic: all elements, frankincense, sandalwood, blue, white, Sunday and Monday

MORRIGAN, ALSO KNOWN AS MORRIGU (CELTIC): Goddess of death, especially on the battlefield—she often appeared as a crow or raven; also associated with magic.

Magic for prophecy, balance, exploring, breaking illusions, seeing painful truths: water element

Gods

APOLLO (GREEK AND ROMAN): One of the most important deities in both Greek and Roman religions—god of prophecy, archery, healing, poetry, and music. Later he became associated with the sun. (His identity was later merged with Hyperion and Helios, who were also sun gods.)

Healing Magic: all elements, frankincense, sandalwood, blue, white, Sunday and Monday

Creativity Magic: all elements, yellow, lavender, Wednesday

CERNUNNOS (CELTIC): His name means "the horned one." A Celtic god worshipped in France and Britain; known as a god of fertility and nature, also wealth and warriors. A male figure with antlers, often depicted sitting in a cross-legged position surrounded by animals; sometimes with a serpent in one hand and a torc (neck ring worn by royalty) in the other. God, priest, or shaman, he is the probable origin of the "Green Man" myth—lord of the animals and god of regeneration. Also associated with abundance. Part man and part beast, he symbolizes the connection with the wild.

Protection Magic: all elements, white, silver, clove, basil, frankincense, rosemary, Sunday

Love Magic: element of water, pink, cinnamon, pine and rose, Friday

Banishing Magic: earth element, black, frankincense, rosemary, Saturday

Fertility Magic: earth and water elements, green, red, geranium, pine, Monday and Sunday

FREYR OR FREY (NORSE): Twin brother of Freya, and one of the principal Norse gods, mainly concerned with fertility and also in control of rain and sunlight—also associated with peace.

Fertility Magic: earth and water elements, green, red, geranium, pine, Monday and Sunday

HERMES (GREEK) AND MERCURY (ROMAN): Messenger god who enjoyed games and playing tricks; associated with crossroads; Mercury also watched over trade and commerce.

Creativity, Money, and Business Magic: all elements, yellow, lavender, Wednesday

LUGH (CELTIC): Irish name for the Celtic sun god, known as Lleu in Wales; also called "the many-skilled."

Strength Magic: earth element, red, frankincense, cinnamon, oak, Sunday and Tuesday

ODIN OR WODEN (NORSE): Chief god of Scandinavian mythology; god of magic and wisdom, battle, and guardian of the underworld. Shape-shifter and protector of young heroes.

Strength Magic: earth element, red, frankincense, cinnamon, oak, Sunday and Tuesday

SATURN (ROMAN): An ancient Italian god of harvest and time—he became the basis for our figure of "father time"—his origin is from his Greek counterpart, Chronos or Cronos/Kronos, whose name means "time." This association with Kronos, one of the primordial deities at the beginning of creation, came about later. Originally, Saturn was the god of sowing in the winter to prepare for next season's harvest. His name is believed to come from the word *saeta*, meaning "seed." Some scholars say his name is Etruscan and its meaning is not clear. What is clear is that he was celebrated during Saturnalia at the time of winter solstice and at cleansing and purification rituals. Kronos also had a festival during mid-winter.

Banishing Magic: earth element, black, frankincense, rosemary, Saturday

THOR (GERMANIC/NORSE): Thunder god, bearing his magic hammer, a mighty protector and guardian. Also guardian of oaths. Our day Thursday is named for him. He is also equated with Jupiter.

Protection Magic: all elements, white, silver, clove, basil, frankincense, rosemary, oak, Sunday

Banishing Magic: earth element, black, frankincense, rosemary, Saturday

ZEUS (GREEK) AND JUPITER (ROMAN): Supreme deity and all-powerful sky god. Often associated with mountains and hilltops.

Strength Magic: earth element, red, frankincense, cinnamon, oak, Sunday and Tuesday

Fertility Magic: earth and water elements, green, red, geranium, pine, Monday and Sunday

Abundance Magic: rose, element of earth, green, gold, purple, silver, basil, cinnamon, dill, Thursday and Sunday

appendix b | Basic Circle-Casting Outline

For those new to the practice of magic, here is an outline to guide you through the process of casting a circle.

Clean the area and create your sacred space by arranging all your supplies. If you wish, perform an energy cleansing by burning incense or sprinkling the area with salt water.

Identify the four cardinal points and place markers at each or light a candle of the corresponding color. Beginning with north,★ move clockwise around the circle. As you do, recite the following for each direction:

> *To the north, I honor the element of earth. Field, forest, stone, and tree—*
> *   hail and welcome!*

★ Some practitioners like to begin in the east, since this is where the sun rises. The choice is yours.

To the east, I honor the element of air. Wind and sky, breath and breeze—
    hail and welcome!
To the south, I honor the element of fire. Sun and flame, warm energy—
    hail and welcome!
To the west, I honor the element of water—river, rain, spring, and sea—
    hail and welcome!

If you choose to invite the presence of deity, do so now, in your own words.

Imagine a circle of light around you—more than just a circle … a sphere, a protective bubble. You're in the center, so part of the sphere is under the floor. Visualize this bubble as being protective and holding your energy until you're ready to release it. You can imagine this circle any way you'd like. I like to envision a sphere of bright blue-white light. Walk around the area three times in clockwise fashion, each time imagining the circle growing stronger. You can use your hand to gesture and imagine the energy flowing from within you to create the circle. After the third time, stop and say:

The circle is cast. I am now between the worlds.

Perform whatever magical work you require. When you are finished, close the circle by thanking each of the elementals and saying "Hail and farewell." Also thank any deity you invited. Go in reverse order from the way you started. If you began in the north and ended with the west, begin now in the west and end with the north, thanking each direction as you go around the circle. Then walk three times counterclockwise, visualizing the circle disappearing. As this happens, also visualize the energy you raised within it being sent out into the universe toward your goal. Say:

The circle is open, but unbroken.

Closing the circle is important to keep unwanted energy from lingering around. It's important for you to ground yourself after you're finished. Simply put, this is an act of dismissing any excess energy. Carrying too much magical energy around with you can make you lightheaded and dizzy. One simple way to ground is to sit on the floor and place your palms on the floor in front of you. Visualize yourself connecting with the earth and excess energy being absorbed by the floor, down into the ground. Having something to eat or drink is another good way to complete the grounding process. Think of it like electricity—wires must be properly grounded for safety, so the energy isn't loose. That's what you're doing here, getting rid of excess energy. You should then clean up your area. Mundane tasks like this are also part of the grounding process.

One of the traditional practices in Wicca is to have "cakes and ale" as part of a magical ritual before closing the circle. This is an act of grounding for the practitioner and also a way to give thanks by "sacrificing" a bit of food and drink to the earth as an offering. In a coven gathering, the food and drink are first blessed by the High Priestess and then shared with the group. Most practitioners just leave a bit of the food (bread, cookies, etc.) outside and pour a bit of the drink (any type of beverage) on the ground, or even in a potted plant.

The circle casting for candle creation is optional. The most important thing is your intent while making the candles, so if this step helps you focus, go ahead and do it. Otherwise, just make sure you're working in sacred space. You can designate the area as special by playing music you enjoy or burning incense. Enjoy the experience. Even if you're just in your kitchen, garage, or basement, do something extra to make the area special. Something out of the ordinary. Don't have the TV on in the background, for example. Wear special jewelry. Take a relaxing bath before working. Have a glass of wine. Do whatever makes you feel special and makes your surroundings feel special as well.

> *I make this sacred space my own,*
> *In this time, within my home.*
> *Clear this place, make it clean,*
> *As I will so mote it be.*

Glossary of Terms

amulet: Something worn or carried for protection, most often a piece of jewelry. See *talisman*.

archetype: As defined by psychologist Carl Jung, types of universal human instincts, impulses, characters, etc., that have become the common idea of myths.

aromatherapy: The use of essential oils from plants to affect well-being. Scents are inhaled or used in bath or massage.

aura: The subtle energy field that is said to surround a person or object.

charge: To mentally project a specific type of energy into an object.

consecration: The act of dedicating an item or place as sacred or to be used for special purpose.

coven: A group of Wiccans or Witches who gather together to celebrate, practice magic, and worship together, usually led by a High Priestess and High Priest. More informal groups are sometimes called circles.

divination: A practice intended to reveal information, future predictions, and so on, often using Tarot cards, a crystal ball, runes, or some other tool.

element: In magic, refers to the four classical elements of earth, air, fire, and water, without which life as we know it would not be possible. Spirit is sometimes considered to be the fifth element.

esbat: Celebrations of the full moon, or other times Wiccans and Witches gather to celebrate and worship.

Hermetic philosophy: A set of practices and philosophies from Hellenistic Egypt that were said to be derived from the wisdom of Hermes Trismegistus, a blend of the Egyptian god Thoth and the Greek god Hermes—both associated with writing and magic. Some say he was a wise prophet.

hex sign: Any type of sign—usually round, painted, and including stars, rosettes, and other designs—that is thought to be magical. Often seen painted on barns and houses by the Pennsylvania Dutch to ward off harmful spirits and keep misfortune at bay.

infusion: An extract made by soaking plant material in warm or hot water.

magic circle: Sacred space created by energy and visualization where magic and rituals are performed.

mandala: In Buddhism and Hinduism, a diagram having spiritual and/or ritual significance. *Mandala* is Sanskrit for "circle."

mantra: A sound, syllable, or words that are repeated like a chant or affirmation. Intended to be used to achieve transformation, from Eastern religious practices.

metaphysics: The philosophical study of the ultimate causes and underlying nature of things.

mortar and pestle: A mortar is a small bowl or dish, usually made of stone or ceramic. The pestle is a tool (a short, thick wand rounded on one end) used to grind herbs or resins in this dish. This image is often used to symbolize a pharmacy.

Neo-Pagan: "New" Paganism, referring to modern polytheistic religious beliefs, including Wicca and modern Witchcraft.

New Age: A term often used to refer to eclectic beliefs and practices that rose to popularity in the United States during the 1960s and 1970s and have evolved into current use. A collection of esoteric and spiritual techniques that blend Eastern and Western philosophies, ancient and modern. Often includes astrology, crystal healing, transcendental meditation, aromatherapy, etc.

occult: Meaning "hidden" or shrouded in mystery.

pantheism: Belief system that sees the universe or nature as the Divine.

projective hand: The hand you use to write, or the hand you use most often. Use this hand to project energy.

receptive hand: The hand you don't write with, or use less often. Used to receive energy.

runes: Ancient writing system originating in northern Europe.

sabbat: Eight sacred times of the year that Wiccans celebrate, based on seasonal changes.

sachet: A small bag often filled with perfumed powder or other scented material, such as dried herbs and flowers.

scrying: Process of divination that involves gazing into a crystal, water, or other medium to see images or symbols.

shaman: Often a tribal medicine man. Someone who practices spiritual and healing arts, divination, and communication with the spirit world.

smudging: Ritual cleansing of an object or space using the smoke of burning herbs and/or resins.

snuffer: A bell- or dome-shaped object, often at the end of a stick or wand, used to extinguish a candle flame.

talisman: Often confused with an amulet, a talisman is an object created to be used for magical purpose in attracting something, such as wealth or good fortune (whereas an amulet is made to repel evil and give protection). Talismans are often created for a specific purpose, while amulets are more general. Both can be carried or worn as jewelry.

Tarot: Card system used for divination.

yin and yang: In Chinese philosophy, yin is "darkness" and yang is "light"—cosmic powers that interact to create everything in the universe. Not literally dark and light, but a union of opposites that depend on each other—light and shadow, moist and dry, masculine and feminine. Yin is the feminine and yang is the masculine.

Sources and Recommended Reading

Altschuler, Daniel R. *Children of the Stars*. New York: Cambridge University Press, 2002.

Aveni, Anthony F. *Behind the Crystal Ball*. Boulder, CO: University Press of Colorado, 2002.

———. *Conversing with the Planets.* Boulder, CO: University Press of Colorado, 2002.

Bently, Peter, ed. *The Dictionary of World Myth.* New York: Facts on File, 1995.

Blake, Jane. *Handmade Candles*. New York: Hearst Books, 1998.

Bowes, Susan. *Life Magic.* New York: Simon & Schuster, 1999.

Bruce-Mitford, Miranda. *The Illustrated Book of Signs and Symbols.* New York: Barnes and Noble Books, 2004.

Cabot, Laurie. *Power of the Witch.* New York: Delacorte, 1989.

Campbell, Joseph, and Bill Moyers. *The Power of Myth.* New York: Doubleday, 1988.

Conway, D. J. *Moon Magick.* St. Paul, MN: Llewellyn Publications, 1995.

Cottrell, Arthur, and Rachel Storm. *The Ultimate Encyclopedia of Mythology.* London: Hermes House, 1999.

Cunningham, Scott. *Cunningham's Encyclopedia of Magical Herbs.* St. Paul, MN: Llewellyn Publications, 1999.

———. *Living Wicca.* St. Paul, MN: Llewellyn Publications, 1993.

———. *Magical Aromatherapy.* St. Paul, MN: Llewellyn Publications, 1999.

———. *Wicca for the Solitary Practitioner.* St. Paul, MN: Llewellyn Publications, 1988.

Curott, Phyllis. *Witch Crafting.* New York: Broadway Books, 2001.

Drew, A. J. *A Wiccan Formulary and Herbal.* Franklin Lakes, NJ: New Page Books, 2005.

Dugan, Ellen. *Book of Witchery.* Woodbury, MN: Llewellyn Publications, 2009.

Freeman, Mara. *Kindling the Celtic Spirit.* New York: Harper, 2001.

Gawain, Shakti. *Creative Visualization.* Mill Valley, CA: Bantam, 1979.

Guiley, Rosemary Ellen. *The Encyclopedia of Witches and Witchcraft,* 2nd edition. New York: Checkmark Books, 1999.

Heinberg, Richard. *Celebrate the Solstice.* Wheaton, IL: Quest Books, 1993.

Holland, Eileen. *The Wicca Handbook.* York Beach, ME: Weiser, 2000.

Hutton, Ronald. *The Triumph of the Moon.* New York: Oxford University Press, 1999.

———. *Stations of the Sun.* New York: Oxford University Press, 1996.

Johnstone, Michael. *The Ultimate Encyclopedia of Spells.* New York: Gramercy Books, 2003.

Jones, Prudence, and Nigel Pennick. *A History of Pagan Europe.* New York: Barnes and Noble Books, 1999.

Joseph Campbell Foundation. *Pathways to Bliss.* Novato, CA: New World Library, 2004.

Judith, Anodea. *Chakra Balancing.* Boulder, CO: Sounds True, 2003.

Jung, Carl G., M. L. von Franz, Joseph L. Henderson, Jolande Jacobi, and Aniela Jaffe. *Man and His Symbols.* New York: Laurel, 1964.

Kluger, Jeffrey. "Is God in Our Genes?" *Time Magazine.* October 25, 2004.

Leeming, David. *Myth: A Biography of Belief.* New York: Oxford University Press, 2002.

Marinoff, Lou. *Plato, Not Prozac!* New York: MJF Books, 1999.

Matthews, Caitlin. *The Celtic Book of Days.* Rochester, NY: Destiny Books, 1995.

Melody. *Love is in the Earth: A Kaleidoscope of Crystals Update.* Wheat Ridge, CO: Earth-Love Publishing, 1995.

Mordord and Lenardon. *Classical Mythology*, 7th edition. New York: Oxford University Press, 2003.

Oswald, Bob. *Discovering Runes.* Edison, NJ: Chartwell Books, 2008.

Parker, Julia, and Derek Parker. *Astrology.* New York: Dorling Kindersley, 2007.

Picton, Margaret. *The Book of Magical Herbs.* New York: Quarto/Barron's, 2000.

Renée, Janina. *By Candlelight.* St. Paul, MN: Llewellyn Publications, 2004.

Riggs-Bergesen, Catherine. *Candle Therapy.* Kansas City, MO: Andrews McMeel Publishing, 2003.

Rogers, Nicholas. *Halloween: From Pagan Ritual to Party Night.* New York: Oxford University Press, 2002.

Sachs, Maryam. *The Moon.* New York: Abbeville Press, 1998.

Shlain, Leonard. *The Alphabet Versus the Goddess.* New York: Viking, 1998.

Simpson, Liz. *The Book of Crystal Healing.* New York: Sterling, 1997.

Stawhawk. *The Spiral Dance.* New York: Harper, 1979.

Summers, Lucy. *The Book of Wicca.* New York: Quarto/Barron's, 2001.

Telesco, Patricia. *Exploring Candle Magick.* Franklin Lakes, NJ: New Page Books, 2001.

Tyson, Neil deGrasse, and Donald Goldsmith. *Origins.* New York: W.W. Norton, 2004.

Valiente, Doreen. *Natural Magic.* Custer, WA: Phoenix, 1975.

Index

theta state, 27

timing, 53, 55–56, 59–60, 66, 80–83, 92, 96, 98, 100, 102, 104, 106, 108, 113, 115–116, 118–119, 123–124, 129

tools, magical, 11, 16, 27, 29, 32, 34, 51, 59, 67, 74–76, 209

trance, 4, 27–28, 39

transformation, 38, 75, 78, 82, 96–97, 108, 135–136, 152–153, 155, 176, 191, 196, 217, 219, 222, 226

Triple Goddess, 114, 194, 215, 223, 225–226

triskele, 192, 194

Uranus (planet), 131, 134, 221

Venus (goddess), 64, 100, 129, 139, 223

Venus (planet), 80, 130, 132–133, 207, 209, 214, 216–217, 222

Virgo, 63, 77, 80, 133, 136, 158, 160

visualization, 18, 24–27, 31–32, 34–35, 41, 48–49, 51, 58, 61, 77, 81–83, 96, 99–102, 105, 107, 117, 124, 126–127, 129, 138, 140, 142, 145–149, 151–155, 157–160, 162, 167–172, 175, 180, 189–190, 209, 216, 232–233

votive candle, 2, 12–17, 19, 21–22, 24, 67, 91, 141, 185–187

wand, 27, 34, 74

water (element), 33, 62–64, 72, 74–79, 83–84, 105, 118, 132, 134–135, 139–141, 151–153, 156, 160–161, 165, 169–172, 175, 182, 184–185, 194–196, 207, 209–211, 214, 216, 223–229, 231–232

wax, 2, 5–6, 10–21, 34–38, 41, 47–49, 52–53, 60, 65, 67–69, 77, 79–83, 91–93, 96–98, 100, 102, 104, 106, 108, 113–114, 116–119, 121–122, 124, 126–127, 129, 131–135, 138, 140–153, 155–162, 164–173, 175, 181–183, 187–188, 196, 213

Wheel of the Year, 77, 86–88, 90, 103, 105

Wiccan Rede, 42

wicks, 10–11, 13–16, 18–20, 48, 67, 98, 129, 141, 145, 149–150, 166, 169, 181–183, 188

winter solstice, 88–89, 92–94, 113, 186, 229

yin and yang, 117, 192, 194

zodiac, 74–77, 114, 124, 127–128, 131, 135, 193

CPSIA information can be obtained at www.ICGtesting.com
Printed in the USA
LVOW01s2320160115

423197LV00001B/1/P